HAPPINESS • SUCCESS • ROMANCE • GOOD FORTUNE • ARE YOU READY FOR YOUR STAR-STUDDED FUTURE?

Whatever you desire can be yours if you just reach out to the stars for guidance. Let Sydney Omarr's unique astrological expertise show you the promise that 1984 holds in store for you with this specially charted, day-by-day horoscope for your sun sign.

With the help of the zodiac you can learn how to make the right decisions at the right time, and you'll be able to put all your assets to work for you every day of the week and every week of the year.

SYDNEY OMARR'S
Day-by-Day Astrological Guide for
SCORPIO
(October 23–November 21)
1984

A SIGNET BOOK

NEW AMERICAN LIBRARY

TIMES MIRROR

SIGNET TRADEMARK REG. U.S. PAT. OFF. AND FOREIGN COUNTRIES
REGISTERED TRADEMARK—MARCA REGISTRADA
HECHO EN CHICAGO, U.S.A.

SIGNET, SIGNET CLASSICS, MENTOR, PLUME, MERIDIAN and NAL BOOKS are published by The New American Library, Inc., 1633 Broadway, New York, New York 10019

First Printing, July, 1983

1 2 3 4 5 6 7 8 9

PRINTED IN THE UNITED STATES OF AMERICA

CONTENTS

INTRODUCTION

Have you ever marveled at the fact that no two human beings are exactly alike? Have you ever been struck by the wide disparity that often exists in both looks and temperament among members of the same family unit? One of the most stunning facts of life is that each of us is a separate, distinct individual—a first-time phenomenon in the history of the world. Human diversity is one of the world's greatest wonders . . . and one of life's greatest potential problems.

Because we are so different, no one yet has been able to devise one simple, fail-safe system for finding success and happiness. Each of us has to find the way through his or her own personal maze, with very few reliable road signs. Here and there we may come upon some crumbs of experience dropped by an older and wiser Hansel or Gretel; but, in the main, we're on our own to tap-dance our way around the innumerable pitfalls each day reveals.

If there is a secret for finding the right path to personal fulfillment, it appears to be self-knowledge. People of great wisdom have been telling us so for eons, and our most time-honored role models tend to be those who dared to plumb their personal depths. Today, self-understanding is the goal of most therapies, from psychoanalysis to hypnotic regression. In effect, these methods say that if we know why we feel, think, and act as we do, we can be in much better control of our lives and destinies. This concept is the theory, and self-understanding is the goal, of contemporary astrology as well.

Modern astrologers know that the horoscope—one's individual astrological imprint—stands alongside other factors such as genetics and early environment in accounting for personal uniqueness. Many astrologers now combine study of their ancient craft with investigation of biological and social sciences, particularly human psychology. There is also a heightened awareness that astrology really was and is a tool for probing the mystery of the human psyche. While shunning the sterile, empty conclusions of the behaviorists, astrologers do in general adhere to the theory that we create what happens to us by how we happen to the world. It is the *why* of our actions that is the key to our destiny.

Then what is the "magic" of the magic wheel of the horoscope? What do astrologers know that is hidden from the rest of us? Quite literally, the astrologer's special talent is fluency in the most ancient language in our solar system—the language of the movements of the sun, moon, and planets in the sky above us, movements observed since the beginning of intelligent life on earth, spoken of since the beginning of oral tradition, recorded since the beginning of written history. By translating this language, astrologers provide us with a wealth of "inside information." Operating on the principle that what goes on above is mirrored in our world below, they crack the celestial code ... giving us extraordinary insights into human behavior, and alerting us to the probable influences on that behavior as the world turns.

The most basic thing astrologers do is to classify people according to their temperaments. The broadest division is by "sun sign"—twelve different ways human beings have been observed to perceive and react to the world. Your sun sign, determined by what segment of the zodiac the sun was moving through during the month you were born, stamps you with the set of characteristics—both "good" and "bad"—that are most easily available to you, though you can choose among them. For instance, Leo's legendary desire to be at the center of things can manifest itself as mere vanity and showiness—or as true leadership ability.

In the main this book deals with your sun sign, because it is the one astrological fact most people know about themselves. Your total "horoscope" (see next section) is much more complex and must be calculated individually. However, your sun sign is still your horoscope's foundation, in terms both of your character and of the probable crossroads you will come to as you go along from day to day.

With that in mind, use this book as a "planning guide" for the year to come. Heed what it has to say about both your potential assets and your avoidable liabilities; check out your compatibility with other astrological personalities; see how you can look for love in the right places; find out which career areas are most likely to yield personal success and fulfillment; learn what time it is for you according to the great celestial clock. And—perhaps most important—use the inside information the daily forecasts give you to plan your moves with precision. It's more than a truism that life is timing, and knowing when to act is often the key to everything.

1. TEST YOUR A.Q. (ASTROLOGY QUOTIENT)

Astrology is enjoying a new vigor as contemporary interest in the ancient subject grows, both in width and in depth. There is a positive awareness that far from being a "new-age" fad, astrology has a long and fascinating past, as well as an active and stimulating present. If you are one of the many people who pride themselves on being "astrology-smart," you can find out just how good a handle you have on the subject by checking your knowledge against the quiz on the next few pages. The questions are those most asked by both the average person and the beginning astrologer; the answers are designed not only to provide information, but also to lay to rest some popular misconceptions.

As the earth gradually slips into the Age of Aquarius, there is an increased openness to "occult" knowledge. One benchmark: There are surprising numbers of people today who know that the word "occult" simply means "hidden" or obscured from view. As astrology discards some of its wrappings, it will also leave behind a great deal of its mystery. Most astrologers welcome the fact that a little light is being shed on their chosen profession, because they are anxious to bring it into the modern world. However, there is another good reason for "opening up" astrology, and that is its incredible richness as a subject of study.

To enter the world of astrology is to encounter myth,

symbol, language, literature, theology, psychology, metaphysics, and philosophy—not to mention science and mathematics. It's unlikely you will ever become an astrologer, or penetrate much below the surface of the subject. However, with the mini-course in these pages, you can increase your A.Q. at least tenfold—and be light years ahead of most people.

How old is astrology?

There are traditions in many parts of the world, including India and China, that as early as 3000 to 2000 B.C. men were observing the heavens and calculating the movement of the planets, which were thought to be gods. Credit for developing an astrological system more or less as we know it is generally given to the astrologer-priests of the Chaldeans in Mesopotamia, starting about 700 B.C. It is from that time that we have actual records of observations of how movements of the bodies in the sky corresponded to events on earth. The Romans picked up on astrology, which they learned from the Greeks, about 300 B.C. However, in Rome astrologers had to compete with other types of sooth-sayers plying their predictive trades. Astrology remained synonymous with astronomy and to some extent theology until many centuries later when astrology became more "personalized." During the Renaissance, astrology experienced a heyday, though certain factions in the church condemned it for being "fatalistic." In the fourteenth and fifteenth centuries, if you were anybody, you had your own personal astrologer. The so-called Age of Enlightenment or scientific era (c. 1600) dealt a pretty heavy blow to astrology, from which it did not begin to recover until the mid to late 1800s. Today, astrology is alive and well, and is beginning to make its peace with some scientifically minded skeptics.

What is the difference between astrology and astronomy?

At one time there was no difference. All astrologers were astronomers (and vice versa) and were accorded a great deal of prestige. With the dawn of the scientific era some two hundred years ago there came a split between the two disciplines, and they went their separate ways. Now the astronomer measures and calculates planetary positions, and the astrologer interprets the data in terms of human life. One of the best statements of the relationship between the two pursuits was made by Ralph Waldo Emerson: "Astrology is astronomy brought to earth and applied to the affairs of men."

What is the zodiac?

The word "zodiac" literally means "circle of animals" and probably was originally used to refer to the constellations, which supplied the names for the twelve signs. For many centuries the word has *not* referred to the constellations, but to an imaginary 360-degree band around the earth which begins at the point where the sun reaches zero degrees, Aries (the vernal equinox and the beginning of the agricultural year). The signs follow each other at 30-degree intervals along the board until the sun reaches 29 degrees of Pisces, the last day of winter. Points along the zodiac are the astrologer's frame of reference, as well as the celestial navigator's.

Why do we say the sun has "moved" into a sign when we know the sun doesn't move?

There is evidence that even the earliest astrologers were aware that the sun is the center of our solar system and that the earth as well as the other planets orbit around it. (One of the gems of ancient knowledge which went into obscurity during the dark ages of man.) We say the sun "moves" because astrology is an observed science which deals with the *apparent* movement of the heavenly bodies from our reference point here on earth. The apparent path of the sun as it "moves" through the signs throughout the year is actually the path of the earth as it orbits the sun. We all use similar terminology when we speak of the sun "coming up" and "going down."

What is a horoscope?

The word "horoscope," which comes from the Greek, literally means "watcher of the hour." As the word is used today, your horoscope is the map an astrologer draws of the positions of the sun and the planets in the heavens at the moment you were born. It is often referred to as your birth chart or natal chart. The word "horoscope" is often loosely used to mean your forecast or prediction for the day, week, or year.

How does an astrologer draw up a chart or horoscope?

The astrologer's basic tool is an ephemeris—an astronomically calculated reference book which gives the exact positions of the sun and the planets with relation to the 360-degree circle of the zodiac for every day of any given year. Using the ephemeris, as well as other reference books such as an atlas, the astrologer computes the positions of the planets exactly, and draws a precise picture of the sky as if he were standing at your birthplace at the moment you took your first breath. The more important work of the astrologer is his *interpretation* of your chart—a complex process requiring much skill and training.

Why is it important to the astrologer to know the time of day you were born?

A horoscope is like a great wheel or pie divided into twelve segments called "houses." Each house indicates a particular sphere of human experience—the self, others,

8

children, work, career, romance, marriage, etc. Within any given twenty-four-hour period, the wheel makes a full cycle, and so boundaries of the house change from minute to minute. What your time of birth tells the astrologer is which houses of the horoscope the planets of your chart fall into—an extremely important factor in determining the action of the planets for you individually. The placement of the sun in the houses is particularly significant, as the sun is "you" in essence— the conscious self. If you know your time of birth within an hour or so, you can find out which "house" is your sun's "home" in a later chapter of this book. In most states, birth times are on record going back quite a number of years. There is generally a Bureau of Vital Statistics which can tell you this information about your birth.

What is most important in astrology—the planets, the signs of the zodiac, or the houses?

All three are about equal in importance when spelling out character or events, but each has a different function. There is a theatrical metaphor that helps to clarify them. Think of the planet as the actor, the sign as the costume and makeup the actor wears, and the house as the particular set against which the action is staged. It is then easier to see that the planet provides the actual action or "event," that the sign the planet is in gives the action its particular color and meaning, and that the house suggests which area of life is being affected.

What does it mean to be "born on the cusp"?

If your birthday falls either at the very beginning or very end of a sign, you are said to be "born on the cusp"—the dividing line between two signs. Contrary to popular belief, "cusp" days vary from year to year, and signs do not always begin or end on the same date (or time). If you are unsure about your birth sign, use the tables on pages 61 to 67, which give the exact day and hour the sun changed signs every month of every year from 1910 to 1975. Though astrologers differ on the subject, the general consensus is that an individual is influenced by only *one* sun sign, no matter how close the call.

Does astrology work? How does it work?

Most people are not satisfied with the answer that astrology works because—on the empirical evidence of thousands of years—it *works*. They quite naturally want more evidence. The advent of the computer has spurred a great many elaborate research projects which may eventually supply enough data to convince some of the skeptical. The more interesting question is *how* astrology works. Within the astrological community there are a number of different schools of thought on the subject, but the prevailing theories tend to be metaphysical rather than strictly scientific. One is that at the moment of our first breath as we take our place in the universe we are "imprinted" with a pattern—the pattern of placement of the sun, moon, and planets in the various zodiacal signs and their relationship to each other at that moment. The imprint becomes both our individual personality and the "road map" for our lives on earth (which can indicate a number of different routes). Few astrologers believe that specific events are foreordained by this planetary pattern; rather, it affects our character and personality which are the key to our actions— and hence our destinies. However, no horoscope indicates unlimited possibilities for the individual. Within the parameters of our given talents and temperament, we are free to make our own decisions. One of the purposes of astrological predictions, such as those found in this book, is to alert the individuals born under a certain sun sign to the influence and possibilities that are in effect at a given time. What actually happens depends on how we react.

Is there any evidence that the planets really influence us?

The first and most obvious evidence that at least one "planet" has a measurable effect on earth's affairs is the influence of the moon. Even schoolchildren know that the gravitational pull of the moon controls the tides; modern research indicates that the moon has a much wider range of measurable effects. For instance, experiments show that cycles of the moon dictate the daily, and often yearly, rhythms of many life forms, including the oyster. No woman will argue that she does not experience a cycle virtually identical with that of the moon. Increasingly doctors schedule surgery away from the time of the full moon because blood has been observed to flow more freely at that time. It is also well documented that hospitals and emergency clinics find an upsurge in mentally distressed people at this critical time of the month. However, it requires a huge mental leap from the moon's evidence to a conclusion that the other planets affect us in some "scientific" or clearly explainable way. One theory is that electromagnetic emanations from the other planets interact with our body chemistry in a way similar to the gravitational pull of the moon—but it remains theory.

Doesn't the discovery of "new" planets change things from an astrological point of view?

Earliest records tell us that astrologer-astronomers have always been aware of seven "planets": the sun (which is actually a star), the moon (which is a satellite of earth), Mercury, Venus, Mars, Jupiter, and Saturn. That lineup did not change until 1781, when Uranus was discovered; then came the discoveries, much later, of Neptune and Pluto. The revelations of these "modern" planets serve to extend astrologers' knowledge rather than to refute it. With the technological ability to compute the positions of Uranus, Neptune, and Pluto at any point in history, astrologers are able to check out their effects on people and events, and actually see new "reasons" for certain phenomena.

Are astrologers psychic?

Some may be, but psychic or extrasensory powers are not required to become an astrologer. The astrologer bases his interpretation of your personality and his predictions for your future on both historical observations and his own perceptions. As they study and practice, astrologers build up their own bank of information about how certain patterns in the horoscope manifest themselves in the lives and the personalities of people. If the astrologer appears to be "psychic" it is usually because he has sharpened his skills to a very high point. An important theory to remember if you visit an astrologer is that astrology is *not* meant to be a guessing game. To give the most helpful and constructive reading, the astrologer has to know certain pertinent facts about your past and present: whether you are married or single, whether you have children, what you do for a living, and so on. The most obvious reason for supplying this kind of data is to let the astrologer know what *is* happening so he can help you figure out how you might change things, on the basis of the influences he sees coming up in your chart.

How can I find an astrologer/study astrology/become an astrologer?

These three questions often run together as a person first becomes conscious of the tremendous value and validity of astrology to our modern lives. The first question is most easily answered. There are several organizations in the United States for practicing astrologers: the American Federation of Astrologers (P.O. Box 22040, Tempe, AZ 85282), the National Astrological Society (Box 75, Old Chelsea Station, New York, NY 10011), and the National Council for Geocosmic Research (200 West 20th Street, New York, NY 10011), to name the most well known. By writing to one of these associations you can get the names of astrologers practicing in your area. At this point there is no certificate or license needed to practice astrology, and astrological competence does vary. Word-of-mouth reference is often the best way to find one. Although there is no substitute for experience, there are any number of gifted young astrologers who are bringing new insights to this ancient art.

If you would like to study astrology, you might find out the names of schools and/or individual instructors near you by inquiring through the same associations, or by checking your local telephone directory. (Unlike "fortune-tellers," astrologers are permitted to advertise in certain states and communities.) As for becoming an astrologer, think long and hard before you take the plunge into serious study. Astrology is a very demanding, highly complex discipline which requires years of dedicated work. It is one subject where a little knowledge can truly be a dangerous thing. The modern astrologer is a kind of counselor, and while there is a strict code of ethics legitimate astrologers adhere to, it is easy for the novice to give the wrong "advice."

What is the Age of Aquarius?

In recent years the so-called "Age of Aquarius" has gotten a lot of press—and some mixed reviews. Here's what astrologers mean when they use the phrase.

13

From our reference point on earth, the vernal equinox (beginning of the zodiac and the seasonal year) appears to "slip backward" year after year—a fact astronomers attribute to the wobble of the earth as it rotates on its axis. For the past two thousand years or so, the zero point has been in the sign of Pisces, but sometime soon it should be entering the sign of Aquarius, where it will be for the next two thousand years: the Age of Aquarius. To astrologers, each twenty-century period is known as a "great age," and each age has been observed to correspond to a different set of historical/sociological conditions here on earth. The exact year when the Age of Pisces ends and the age of Aquarius begins is a matter of dispute. Judging by such revolutionary movements as equal rights and women's liberation (typical of Uranus-ruled Aquarius), some astrologers believe we have already entered the new age. Others say we are in a period of transition, and that these movements are "early warnings" of the tremendous social and cultural changes to come. Some things that can be said to typify the Age of Aquarius are group consciousness, radical technological advances, the equalizing of all members of society, a feeling of brotherhood, and an emphasis on reason rather than faith. This last is one major point of difference between the new age and the age of Pisces, which corresponds with the Christian era.

Are there different kinds of astrology?

Astrology as we know it grows out of western tradition, and differs in a number of ways from the astrology practiced in India and China. Even within "western" astrology there are a number of schools of thought, but their differences are too subtle and complex to be of interest to the beginner. What is useful to know is that there are different branches within the western astrology that is generally practiced here.

When an astrologer does your horoscope, he is practicing "natal" astrology—which deals with your moment of birth, and how the pattern of the planets affects your growth and development as a human being. Natal astrology can deal with the birth of anything, from a person to a company to a country.

An astrologer might also practice "mundane" astrology, which deals with affairs of state, world politics, and social and economic conditions. When asked to answer a specific question about the probable outcome of any matter, the astrologer might employ the "horary" technique. "Horary" means hour, so a chart is set up for the moment the question is asked. The astrologer divines the answer by interpreting the message of that chart. The principle of "asking the cosmos" at a particular point in time also underlies the *I Ching* and Tarot card readings. "Electional" astrology is a variation on this theme. If you want to know when is the right time to get married, start a business, ask for a raise, have a baby, etc., the astrologer will use a trial-and-error technique to arrive at the right date and time for you. Electional astrology is related to locational astrology, which can theoretically tell you the best choice of geographic location for you or your project.

Within "natal" astrology, the branch most of us are familiar with and will find most pertinent, there are also a couple of subdivisions. "Synastry," which literally means "stars together," is the art of comparing the birth charts of two people to ascertain the nature of the relationship and how it is likely to work in the long run. Many people consult astrologers for synastry charts before they marry. Medical astrology also has a long and prestigious history. The birth or natal chart is a diagnostic tool for practitioners of this art, who can pinpoint or anticipate specific health problems from it. In the strong words of Hippocrates, who is generally regarded as the father of medicine and whose ethical theories guide physicians even today: "He who does not understand astrology is not a doctor but fool." The branch of natal astrology that deals with our immortal rather than temporal lives is called "esoteric" astrology. The birth chart is regarded as a guide to spiritual evolution, and there is usually a strong emphasis on both Christian theology and such oriental ideas as reincarnation and "karma"—a doctrine which explains good and evil in terms of the carryover we bear from previous lifetimes.

2. WHY A SIGN?—THE ELEMENTS AND QUALITIES

There's one aspect of astrology most people agree upon: It's fun. Human beings love to "type" other human beings, and astrology offers a neat and benign system—benign because it allows us to point out other people's foibles without attributing them to sex, race, religion, country of origin, or any other factor that might imply prejudice. Astrology is completely fair: You're overly emotional because you're a Cancer, not because you're the youngest child; you're stubborn and pigheaded because you're a Taurus, not because of where your parents came from; you're an oversexed home-wrecker because you're a Scorpio, not because you totally lack self-control. By the same token, we can flatter ourselves by assuming we possess the better characteristics of our own sun sign: "I'm a Libra, so naturally I must be sweet and pleasant all the time"; "I couldn't have made that mistake, because I'm a careful and conscientious Virgo"; "My Sagittarian sun may make me sloppy, but it gives me energy to burn." When someone poses the question "What is the best sign in the Zodiac?" you can bet that the expected answer is the one the question poser was born under.

But even allowing for such harmless distortions, "what's my sign" is an amazingly easy game to play, and most people can become rather good at it. What's missing in parlor-game astrology is the "why" of the signs, which is essential to really understanding them.

A Sign Is a Symbol

The twelve signs of the zodiac are associated with twelve different representative "pictures"—most of them animal, like the Aries ram, Taurus bull, and Leo lion; some of them human, like the Aquarian water-bearer and Gemini twins; one, the Sagittarian Centaur, half man half animal; and one inanimate—the scales of Libra. Each sign also has a "glyph" or shorthand marking that is used to designate it, such as the familiar horns of the ram. Are we to take these pictures literally and describe the signs in terms of such limited parameters as animal behavior? No. A zodiac sign is a symbol, and like all symbols, it stands for a complex idea not easily expressed in words—certainly not a few words. Think of the cross, one of our most powerful symbols, and the richness of associations it carries with it. The swastika is another example; contrast it with our familiar symbol of the American flag. Some symbols, such as the swastika and American flag, cause different responses in different people. Not so with the signs; they form a symbol system that is mutually agreed upon and has been for centuries. And each sign-symbol carries a wealth of history, tradition, and meaning.

Just as modern science tends to support the view that there is nothing random in the universe, astrologers know there is nothing arbitrary about the designations of certain characteristics to each of the zodiac sign-symbols. Underlying everything there is a beautifully integrated and perfectly logical system of interlocking parts: the elements and the qualities.

Why Twelve Signs?

If you assign each of the four elements—fire, earth, air, water—to all of the three qualities—cardinal, fixed, mutable—you come up with twelve combinations. Conversely, if you assign each of the three qualities to all of the four elements, you get the same number of combinations: twelve—the twelve signs of the zodiac. (Interesting number, 12. It keeps on turning up throughout myth, religion, and tradition. The twelve tribes of Israel, the twelve days of Christmas, the twelve apostles.)

The Greeks, with their passion for order, were the ones who pulled together the centuries of astrological tradition and created the neat and tidy system we now use for arranging the twelve signs of the zodiac according to the four elements and three qualities. Here's how they combine:

	Cardinal	Fixed	Mutable
Fire	Aries	Leo	Sagittarius
Earth	Capricorn	Taurus	Virgo
Air	Libra	Aquarius	Gemini
Water	Cancer	Scorpio	Pisces

Fire, Earth, Air, and Water

The concept of elements probably sprang naturally from early man's experience of the world and his attempts to categorize all that he saw in it, both material and nonmaterial. Comparing the ancients' notion that the four elements made up all things with our modern knowledge that there are actually more than a hundred chemical elements is as pointless as comparing eggs with apples. The early thinkers made no distinction between the solid "real" world and one's experience of that world. The elements fire, earth, air, and water might have more properly been called attributes—of a thing or a person. For instance, if something was experienced as hot rather than cold, sharp rather than dull, active rather than passive, it was said to partake primarily of the fire element. Apply those attributes to certain human personalities, and see how aptly they fit.

In Renaissance times the elements became the "humors," and were applied exclusively to personality. Fire corresponded to the humor "choler"; we still use it today in our word "choleric" (angry). Earth was the humor bile, and an excess led to a melancholy disposition. Air was the humor blood, and too much led to an overly sanguine (or rosy) outlook on life. Water was phlegm, and carried with it a personality as soggy and phlegmatic as it sounds. Shakespeare's dramas are peopled with portraits of the humors: Hamlet, the melancholy Dane, is a prime example.

Just as the elements or humors are key to the delineation of character, they play a vital role in interpersonal relationships. Though the matter of compatibility is more complex, the manner in which the elements of two people's sun signs combine with each other gives a startlingly accurate clue to how those people will get along. The most productive way to think of the astrological elements is as different kinds of energies, or as different ways of perceiving and responding to the world. There is an uncanny correspondence between the elemental or "humor" types and current descriptions of personality types as determined by psychological testing.

Fire corresponds to the "intuitive" personality type. Fire-sign people (Aries, Leo, Sagittarius) do not necessarily have clairvoyant ability, and none is implied by the word "intuitive." Rather, fire people are future-oriented, and prefer to see things not as they are, but as they could be. A visionary quality, enthusiasm, and optimism are three of the most delightful attributes that can often be assigned to people born under Aries, Leo, and Sagittarius.

The easiest way to remember what the element fire represents in terms of personality is to actually visualize it. Fire warms, radiates heat, aspires upward. Fire is spirit, animation, the life principle, which gives a strong sense of personal identity. Too much fire in a personality can translate into self-centeredness.

Just as fire appears to be constantly in motion, fire people are usually on the move, both literally and figuratively. There is a dynamism in fire people which initiates activity—in themselves and in other people. But there is an inherent instability in fire as well. Fire is difficult to contain, and correspondingly, fire people demand more freedom than most, and tend to chafe under restriction. The reactions of fire people are rarely tepid; they tend toward the "hotter" emotions, with all that implies.

It is not difficult to visualize the interaction of fire-sign people with those born into a different element. The air signs "fan" the fire signs and thereby intensify fire's inherent characteristics. Earth people can suffocate fire, or at least make it burn less brightly. As for the water signs, the interaction is fairly obvious: Water puts fire out.

Earth people operate on their sense perceptions: If they can see it, touch it, hear it, it is real. These are the pragmatists of the zodiac, and their reaction to things is often quite literal. The earth element adds practicality to any horoscope. For those born under an earth sign (Taurus, Virgo, Capricorn), a practical turn of mind can be a saving grace—or a cross to bear. Just as you would expect, earth gives a solid foundation to anything, and earth-sign people are often "builders"—of houses, projects, families, whatever. The earth element, according to its nature, often adds a "nurturing" quality to the personality which can be endearing. However, earth can often take away from the imagination. If one sees the world only as it is, it is difficult to carry out visions and dreams . . . or to understand the dreams of others.

If you can visualize a mound of earth pressing down upon a person, you will have an idea of why the earth element is often associated with depression, or at least a lack of joy and spontaneity in the personality. For earth people, life is lived at a pretty basic level, and creature comforts are usually mightily appreciated. This is the reason the earth signs are often dismissed as "materialistic." Not so; what they want is form and substance in their lives. Security—especially emotional—is paramount, and any threat to it makes earth-sign people anxious. On the other hand, just as earth is solid, it is patient, and can wait for things to mature—as fire cannot. The most compatible element for earth is water, because there is a natural synergy between them. Earth/water combinations may not make the world's most sparkling couples, but they can be some of the most lasting relationships.

Air is the "lightest" of the four elements, humors, or psychological types. Fire may be ebullient and outgoing, but air is more peripatetic and social. Air-sign people (Libra, Aquarius, Gemini) act out of the "thinking" principle. From this premise one might make the assumption that people born into the air signs are more intelligent than others. This is not necessarily so. What the "thinking" mode of personality entails is making connections between things and people, linking past to present and future, perceiving the world in a "linear" or logical way. In terms of brain function, it is highly probable that the air signs tend to exhibit more left-brain (rational) than right-brain (intuitive) activity.

As personalities, air-sign people seem able to be objective with less effort than other people, and more of the time. At the extreme, this can amount to total dispassion, and a seeming lack of warmth. The sociability of air-sign people derives from the nature of air itself: Air circulates, air is everywhere, air carries people, things, and ideas with it. As air is the "associating" and "connecting" element, it is the "communicating" element as well. An astonishing number of air-sign people end up in the communication trades: journalism, television, radio, writing of all kinds.

Because air has the ability to be objective, air-sign people can suffer from emotional blocks. Becoming entangled in and constricted by intense emotions is usually anathema to the air signs. The end result of this aversion is a sometimes unfortunate detachment, and difficulty in forming lasting relationships. To make air concentrate on one thing for very long is more difficult than holding nectar in a sieve. The most comfortable companion for an air-sign person is an earth-sign person, because both have a logical or practical turn of mind. The combination of air sign with fire sign is more exciting, but also more unstable.

Water is the "deepest" element, in every sense of the word. Water-sign people (Cancer, Scorpio, Pisces) look at and interpret the world in terms of their emotions; they are the natural "feelers" of the zodiac. The feeling

23

nature of the water signs can generate tremendous creativity in all the art forms, and in life itself. Conversely, it can cause great pain—to the water-sign person himself and to others. Water penetrates; it seeps into and permeates everything. Water has considerable power when harnessed; unharnessed it can spell disaster. Water is the opposite of air, emotional where air is logical, more right-brain (intuitive) than left-brain (rational). One of the "mysterious" properties water can lend to a water-sign personality is the ability to sense what less "sensitive" souls cannot. Water-sign people can often seem to possess powers of precognition; many actually do. However, water's premonitions are often nothing more than vague forebodings about problems that never materialize. Water-sign people generally tend to take life rather seriously; perhaps they are aware, even unconsciously, of the megaton effect of their emotions—both on themselves and on others. Such power is not to be taken lightly.

It's one step from the seriousness of water to the observation that water people can be "heavy." Sometimes they are heavy in the literal sense, but more often in the sense of being less than lighthearted companions. As in all cases, the degree of "heaviness" depends on the total horoscope, rather than just the sun sign; but in general this is the case. Just as water signs tend to gravitate naturally toward the "comfortable" earth signs, they are often mistrustful of the air signs, and downright fearful of the volatile fire signs. Water may put fire out, but fire can potentially make water disappear into thin air. Aside from creativity, the most positive attribute often found in the water signs is the nurturing quality. People often turn toward the water signs in times of distress—to be lulled and rocked as in the fluid of the womb, or "cleansed" by the mystical "purifying" effect of water.

24

The Qualities

The astrological qualities—cardinal, fixed, and mutable—are the missing parts of the puzzle that, when filled in, reveal the twelve zodiacal signs in all their individuality. Each represents a kind of energy, movement, or direction. How precisely does a quality affect an element and combine to become a sign? It is clear when you add quality to element and see how the specific sign emerges.

Cardinal derives from the Latin word for the hinge that permits a door to open. It is appropriately descriptive of the *initiatory* nature of the four cardinal signs: Aries, Cancer, Libra, and Capricorn. Cardinal signs *start* things—each according to its element—and it is no coincidence that they are the signs that "open" each of the four seasons of the year. The cardinal movement is forward, and the direction is straight ahead.

However their energy manifests itself, cardinal signs are movers and shakers, and you will very often find them in the position of "moving force" behind enterprises.

Cardinal quality + *Fire* element = *Aries*
Aries is the most cardinal of the cardinals, coming appropriately at the very opening of the entire zodiac. Like all fire signs, Aries is active and dynamic; as a cardinal sign, Aries often puts that energy into starting things—sometimes finishing little. Even so, people rally round this sign. You are aware in the presence of Aries that there's a natural leader among you; just where he will take you is another matter.

25

Cardinal quality + *Water* element = *Cancer*
The reason Cancer is often able to overcome the water signs' tendency to shy away from the new is that it partakes of the cardinal quality. Cancer may be fearful, yet Cancer moves forward. It should be no surprise that Cancer, so often described as a domestic stay-at-home, is a sign that turns up frequently on the "most successful" list in business and professions.

Cardinal quality + *Air* element = *Libra*
Libra can be another surprising sign—again, because of its cardinality. If your natural penchant is to initiate things, you can't stay on the fence forever. The problem is that affable Libra's strong forward direction is often masked. Desiring to please all and offend no one, Libra can steal the prize and run away with it while you aren't looking.

Cardinal quality + *Earth* element = *Capricorn*
The sign that opens the winter season is often labeled "materialistic." As a cardinal sign, Capricorn moves forward; as an earth sign, Capricorn moves steadily toward the more solid and tangible things of this world. Capricorn's cardinal direction is possibly the most powerful, though Capricorn is less flamboyant than Aries and less calculated than Libra.

Fixed is the quality of the signs that fall in the middle of each season. It goes something like this: The cardinal signs start the action, and the fixed signs consolidate the position. As the word implies, the fixed signs are more stable in their way than either the cardinal or the mutable signs. Because the motion or direction of fixed signs is basically static, centrifugal, or "in place," it is also much more difficult to move, change, or unseat them. The fixed signs are sometimes called the "executive" signs, with good reason.

Fixed quality + *Fire* element = *Leo*
The reason Leo is often extolled as the ideal manager or parent is that this active, warm fire sign burns with a "fixed" or steady heat. Leo stands in the center, and all else pivots around him; you always know where Leo stands. The notable loyalty of Leo also derives from the fixed quality: Once Leo's light shines on you, it will shine forever.

Fixed quality + *Earth* element = *Taurus*
Why is Taurus often described as stubborn? Simple: It's even harder to move the solid earth of Taurus because it is "fixed" in one place. However, when you combine the palpable element earth with the unmoving quality of fixity, you come up with a pretty sturdy character, and one to be counted upon.

Fixed quality + *Water* element = *Scorpio*
The tremendous reserve of many Scorpios can be attributed to the fact that Scorpio is a "fixed" sign. Water's depth of feeling and emotion is tightly contained in one place, and virtually immovable. What this also means is that Scorpios tend toward grudge-keeping and possessiveness; they hold on to ideas and people to the death.

Fixed quality + *Air* element = *Aquarius*
The Aquarian tends to be much less a will o' the wisp than the other air signs, Gemini and Libra. People born under the fixed air sign can better concentrate their abilities—both social and communicative. Their ideas are often both lofty and

sound at one time; fixity gives a firm base for logic. Aquarians often display these tendencies as social reformers and political activists.

Mutable is virtually a synonym for "flexible." The signs that fall at the end of each season are beginning to feel the necessity to move out of the way for the next cardinal sign. The mutable signs' motion is a kind of spiral, or a zigzag pattern resembling broken-field running. Naturally this makes the mutable signs more adaptable than the other signs of the same element, a most valuable asset in social relationships. Unfortunately, mutability also makes these signs a bit less stable and reliable.

Mutable quality + *Fire* element = *Sagittarius*
Sometimes rash and as easily riled as the other fire signs, Sagittarius is more able to forgive and forget than Aries or Leo. Mutable signs "bend." Sagittarians can sometimes bend others out of shape by erratic behavior and "spaced-out" episodes. The reason: their fiery visions come so thick and fast it is difficult for some Sagittarians to communicate them clearly or stick with them for long.

Mutable quality + *Earth* element = *Virgo*
All the earth signs tend toward anxiety, but mutable Virgo can be the most anxious of all. Virgos constantly shift attention from practical concern to practical concern, often causing themselves endless worry. There is a constant need to make this world and everything in it better, more workable, closer to perfect.

Mutable quality + *Air* element = *Gemini*
Since air is constantly circulating anyway, Gemini's mutable or "flexible" quality makes this air sign

28

appear flighty at times. On the other hand, an easygoing manner and genial adaptability make Gemini one of the most delightful companions in the zodiac. A super ability to connect with lots of ideas often makes Gemini a prolific writer, particularly of comedy.

Mutable quality + *Water* element = *Pisces*
The flowing, merging, fluid character of water as both symbol and reality is emphasized in Pisces to the point of taking over the personality. The Piscean's often deserved reputation for unreliability is an unfortunate manifestation of this element/quality combination. On the plus side, however, Pisces' malleability is a fantastic boon to the actor, who must project constantly changing emotions, and to the therapist, who must grasp and interpret them.

3. WHAT SEX IS YOUR SIGN?

A little more than a decade ago, the women's liberation movement erupted on our social scene and changed the way we regard "women's place." More recently, "house husbands" and other nontraditional occupations have appeared, liberating males from stereotypes. This sex-role revolution is one factor leading many to believe we have already entered the "Age of Aquarius," when accepted modes of living will seem to turn upside down. Are we witnessing chaos, or is this gradual closing of the gender gap a return to the way things were meant to be? Once again, astrology has something revealing and cogent to say.

The "Third Sex"

There is an ancient astrological myth that contends there were originally three sexes—male, female, and androgyne. This last was a perfect balance of male and female. Created by the gods as children of the sun, moon, and earth, the three sexes had varying degrees of power by virtue of their parental heritage. The androgynes, possessing both sun (male) and moon (female) characteristics, were the most powerful, and therefore the most threatening to Zeus. Instead of destroying the androgynes, he decided to "split" them

30

into male and female segments. Since then, the myth tells us, the two sexes as we know them have wandered the earth looking for their other and sometimes better half. From this ancient wisdom, revealed as many truths are through myth, we can draw the conclusion that "androgyny" is the desired human condition, and that all of us suffer by our one-sex-to-a-person state.

It is important to establish that we are not talking of sex in the physical, bodily sense, but of *gender*—that is, the qualities of maleness and femaleness as they manifest themselves in outlook and attitudes. The bisexual is not the same as the androgyne, whose nature contains both male and female attributes in perfect balance. Some claim that Jesus Christ was the prototypical androgyne, capable of both great force and great mercy.

The Sex of the Signs

The zodiac is divided into male and female signs. It starts with a masculine sign, Aries, and continues with Taurus, a feminine sign. The subsequent signs alternate male and female throughout the rest of the zodiac.

Masculine signs		Feminine signs	
Aries	Libra	Taurus	Scorpio
Leo	Aquarius	Virgo	Pisces
Sagittarius	Gemini	Capricorn	Cancer

In astrological and other "occult" tradition, the first and primal division of all things is into the polarities, or opposites: masculine and feminine. Everything in the universe partakes of either the male/Yang/active/"plus" principle or the female/Yin/passive/"minus" principle. The polarities are *complementary*, each necessary to the existence of the other. Far from representing a "better" or "worse," each combines with the other to form a perfect whole. The words "positive" and "negative" are another way of expressing the fundamental meaning of polarity, and the photograph is a useful image. The photograph itself is the positive; it is taken from and made possible by the negative. The two are different parts of the same reality. The difference is that the positive is the "light," more visible, more affirming part, and the negative the "dark" and more or less silent part.

The original symbol of the masculine polarity was the sun, so part of maleness is living in the direct light of day, the "outer world," so to speak, and utilizing the direct, left-brain mode of perception. The archetypal symbol of the feminine polarity is the moon, so, correspondingly, femaleness means living in the reflected light of the sun, dwelling in the "inner world," drawing upon "dark," unconscious, right-brain insights.

If these definitions are beginning to sound like our contemporary stereotypes of "the man" and "the woman," it is no accident. But why are some signs masculine and some signs feminine? A look at the elements gives some clues. The fire and air signs are masculine by virtue of their outer-directed, outgoing, initiating, dynamic nature; they dwell on the "light" side of the cosmic equation. The earth and water signs are feminine because in general they are less flamboyant, more inner-directed, "softer," more indrawn. Their nature corresponds to the "dark" or negative side of that same equation. As in photography, it is the positive we see most clearly as opposed to the negative.

To sum up the root meanings of "maleness" and "femaleness":

Masculine	Feminine
Yang	Yin
Active	Passive
Plus	Minus
Positive	Negative
Outer	Inner
Conscious	Unconscious
Left-brain-oriented	Right-brain-oriented
Solar	Lunar
Assertive	Retiring
Self-expressive	Self-repressive
Direct	Indirect
Straightforward	Subtle

And on and on, into any other "polarities" you can name, from hot/cold to rough/smooth to hard/soft.

It should by now be obvious why the androgynes were considered both close to perfect and more powerful than their one-sex sisters and brothers. Earth's original "third sex" had the whole range of maleness and femaleness at its fingertips, and could draw easily upon *both* sides of the cosmos—be both the positive and the negative of the photograph at will. In our limited one-sex-to-a-person world it is harder to achieve that balance and hence that power, but it is nevertheless available to anyone, male or female, regardless of physical sex or zodiacal sun sign.

Right-Sex vs. Wrong-Sex

Since the characteristics of your sun sign are the ones most accessible to you in directing your life and your destiny, the designation of signs as "male" or "female" seems to point to a dilemma: What happens when you are born into a sign opposite to your physical sex?

The bad news is that almost inevitably there is a measure of psychic discomfort. The male-sign woman and the female-sign man often feel they do not "fit in their own skin." For instance, fire-sign and air-sign females, while usually successful in the business and professional worlds, often have difficulty playing the traditional female role in relationships. Correspondingly, water-sign and earth-sign males may assert themselves badly, and secretly desire to refrain from the competition that daily life makes necessary.

The good news for wrong-sex-sign people is that they are much more able to close the "gender gap" within them and evolve toward wholeness, or androgyny. Masculine-sign men may find it easier to be "typically male," and feminine-sign women to be "typically female," but all too often they are one-sided—overly attuned to the masculine or feminine vibrations of the universe. In our role-changing world, it is far from a compliment to be described as "all man" or "all woman."

The road to male/female completeness is made rockier by social conditioning. Boys are obviously endowed physically with the outer "male" part of the connection and girls with the perfect female "socket," and this tends to categorize their roles from the start. In spite of the great strides made by both men and women in recent years, sex-typing is still an unfortunate fact of contemporary life—unfortunate because it imposes a false limitation on our total capabilities as human beings. Astrology offers some interesting ways to develop your "missing half" and come closer to total personhood. One route is via the sibling system.

The Sibling System

The twelve signs of the zodiac, from Aries through Pisces, not only alternate sex, they also represent a "growing-up" process from childhood through old age. That means each astrological sign has an older "brother" or "sister." For instance, Aries, the youngest sign, represents the primal urge to be, the headlong rush into life. Big sister Taurus provides the balance, with less activity, more stability, the urge to nurture rather than to sow. Feminine Pisces, the last and "oldest" sign, is theoretically the wisest, having accumulated the whole of human experience. World-weary Pisces, therefore, looks ahead to young Aries for rejuvenation, and the round starts again.

Since one can meet as many immature Pisces people as "grown-up" Aries people, it is wise not to take the ages of the signs too literally. However, in attempting to overcome "gender gap," it can be extremely helpful for anyone to look to his or her older sibling. Whether you are born into a sign of the "right sex" or the "wrong sex," there are valuable lessons to be learned by observing the sign that comes directly after your own.

Aries:	*Polarity, Taurus:*
Masculine Fire	*Feminine Earth*

The Male: Your constant itch to get things moving can make you feisty and unnecessarily abrupt. Look to Taurus to cultivate patience and develop the ability to bide your time. Your "fast-start" syndrome would bear much better results if you learned to build things one brick at a time, the way Taurus does. Also, your interpersonal relationships might go more smoothly if you learned how to give some Taurean TLC.

The Female: Your Taurus sister instinctively knows when to take a back seat, hence often fares better in affairs of the heart than you do. You can make men feel they've got to win to win you; observe how subtly Taurus deals with her competitive urge. Don't be concerned about practicing passivity. Your sign has endowed you with enough get-up-and-go for two people. Don't lose your "buddy-buddy" tomboy charm in the process, however.

Taurus:	*Polarity, Gemini:*
Feminine Earth	*Masculine Air*

The Male: You may sometimes feel at a disadvantage in the presence of more flamboyant peers. The easiest way for you to even up the situation is to get a bit more verbal. You've got plenty of good ideas that rest on a firm foundation; learning to put them across with some wit and sparkle like Gemini could put you in the driver's seat. Never underestimate your powers of attraction: Your soft-edge sun sign makes you especially attractive to women, not to mention dogs and children.

The Female: You may be too much of the ideal woman for your own good. For one thing, men may take advantage of your patience and make you wait, certain you'll always be there. Take a lesson from more assertive Gemini, and turn the tables—even at the risk of a relationship. Your intense sexuality guarantees you'll never lack a partner. However, your Gemini sister does a few things better than you do; watch the way she circulates and self-promotes, both on the job and on the town.

Gemini: *Polarity, Cancer:*
Masculine Air   *Feminine Water*

The Male: With your skim-the-surface air, you can come across as "brittle." Take a leaf from Cancer's book and try occasionally to be the "strong, silent type." As popular as you may be, you may not be eligible for the best-partner award, on either the home or the office front. Get in touch with some of Cancer's warmth and sensitivity; the Cancer male knows how to do it without getting overly sentimental.

The Female: Gemini women are usually highly visible—and audible. However, they are not always soft to the touch, in a manner of speaking. Your Cancerian sister has her own problems, but this is not usually one of them. Watch how she uses her Cancerian sensitivity to make people feel comfortable with her. As a female in a male sign, you've got an edge, however. You can compete with the best of them—but your "soft side" should never be too far away.

Cancer: *Polarity, Leo:*
Feminine Water   *Masculine Fire*

The Male: There is a saying that Cancer fathers make the best mothers. The why of it is simple: As a male, the Cancerian is programmed to be authoritative; as a Cancer, he is instinctively attuned to the attributes of the feminine polarity, including the urge to nurture and protect. This is a pretty powerful combination in any area of life, but the self-doubting Cancer male could use a large dose of Leo's instinctive self-assurance.

The Female: In the Cancer female it is possible to find a living example of the often-parodied Jewish mother,

37

regardless of ethnic origin. Where the male Cancer can direct with authority, the female Cancer may manipulate with emotionalism—even unwittingly. Her more self-assured Leo sister rallies people round her by being somebody they can lean on. The Cancer woman should never forget her sign is a cardinal one—which means that, like Leo, she has it in her to lead instead of merely follow.

Leo:	*Polarity, Virgo:*
Masculine Fire	*Feminine Earth*

The Male: In the Leo male the fires of idealism and ambition may burn so brightly that he neglects the less glamorous realities of a situation. The feminine sign Virgo—his astrological older sister—has the "womanly" attribute of sitting back and reflecting, picking up the possible flaws that can lead to a downfall for Leo. For some women, Leo males are not hard to resist: They come on so strong it's a turn-off. The retiring quality of feminine Virgo is a good model to follow for counterbalance.

The Female: Strong, loyal Leo, with all its leadership qualities, is a natural to find among women executives. Leo women can be "the boss" with little effort. On the other hand, they can lack insight into the more subtle factors of dealing with employees, peers, and even their own bosses. Leo's Virgo sister is far more canny, always keeping her eye on the ball. Leo women may succeed in business without trying, but in love it's a different matter. Giving out with a fiery rush of emotion right at the start can lead to disillusionment. Older sister Virgo is disillusioned from the start.

Virgo:
Feminine Earth

Polarity, Libra:
Masculine Air

The Male: Here's a case where "gender gap" can have fairly serious consequences. The Virgo male is often the perfect underling, the perpetual follower, the legendary "bridesmaid" who never becomes a bride. The feminine urge to self-repress meshes too perfectly with the Virgo nature, and it is quite difficult for the male Virgo to tap his self-assertive natural resources. Big brother Libra is an ideal role model, since he can move ahead of others and achieve without ruffling feathers or becoming abrasive.

The Female: Obviously the above applies in spades to the Virgo female. She can suffer from the painful anxiety that comes of trying to be the perfect servant in an imperfect world. Whatever her occupation or role, unfounded fears of failing can amount to paranoia. The lesson to be learned from Libra is objectivity: Virgo women should learn to say, "what is really going on here . . . what is really expected of me?" The other Libra secret for Virgo: Relax and take time to smell the roses.

Libra:
Masculine Air

Polarity, Scorpio:
Feminine Water

The Male: As a sign, Libra is a bit of an anomaly—masculine, yet oddly "soft-edge." The paradox stems from Libra's rulership by the lovely planet Venus. As a result, Libra males have a great blend of natural and astrological equipment. Where they can come a cropper is in appearing to lack conviction, about both ideas and people. Libra's lack of intensity has its polar opposite in Scorpio, the sign the male Libra should look to for guidance. Along with intensity, Scorpio possesses a natural tenacity, something lackadaisical Libra could use a dose of.

The Female: The planet Venus also comes to the aid of the female Libra, giving her a romantic aura that is often irresistible. Yet airlike Libra can resist very well, often too well. The female Libran can suffer from lack of involvement—a sometimes disturbing tendency to remain cool when others heat up. Both in romance and in business, Libra females might fare better if they emulated "older" Scorpios, who fling themselves into the fray, becoming totally involved, living life both more intensely and more interestingly.

Scorpio: *Polarity, Sagittarius:*
Feminine Water   *Masculine Fire*

The Male: The emotionalism of the water signs has more serious consequences in Scorpio, who all too often can "play the heavy," usually by holding on to everything—including the "darker" emotions like jealousy and suspicion. The male Scorpio's ideal role model is Sagittarius, who is far more able to let go and adopt a philosophical attitude toward life's inevitable disappointments. "Heavy" can also describe Scorpio's mood a great deal of the time; a healthy dose of Sagittarian optimism could do wonders.

The Female: Generally more liked by men than by women, the Scorpio female can overplay her own sex role. Scorpio women sometimes fancy themselves *femmes fatales* because of the emotional episodes that may occur with regularity in their relationship lives. Truth is, men as well as women eventually turn off, looking for a lighter partner. Scorpio's older-brother sign, Sagittarius,

40

offers an answer: Start shooting for the stars instead of staring at your navel.

Sagittarius: Polarity, Capricorn:
Masculine Fire   Feminine Earth

The Male: This likable and lively sign produces some of the friendliest types in the zodiac. The Sagittarian male may run into problems as a manager, however, when he finds it necessary to lay down the law. His uppermost concern is likely to be congeniality rather than productivity. The next sign, Capricorn, is much tougher—and, therefore, a good person for Sagittarius to watch. Although a touch less interesting, Capricorn has more staying power in relationships than Sagittarius as well.

The Female: The Sagittarian woman can be confusing to the opposite sex: Does she want to be a buddy or a sweetheart? Usually the Sagittarian female herself does not know; the only thing she's sure of is that she doesn't want to be fenced in, because life is so full of marvelous possibilities. Older-sister sign Capricorn can chime in sensibly with the most male of male conversations, but she never forgets the skin she's in. A dash of Capricorn stability could be a great boon to the slapdash Sagittarian's modus operandi, as well.

Capricorn: Polarity, Aquarius:
Feminine Earth   Masculine Air

The Male: One of the zodiac's more solid citizens, the Capricorn male can usually be counted on, no matter what the duty or obligation. People sometimes wish he were a bit less predictable and a lot more exciting, however. While Capricorn is a consummate doer and achiever, the feminine nature of the sign makes the Capricorn male rather self-repressive. Aquarius, his sibling sign, can strike a balance. Mature Aquarians are rarely truly unconventional, but they know how and when to stray from the beaten track and make life more interesting.

The Female: A natural "success sign," Capricorn breeds some of our most achieving female executives; it also produces some pretty lonely ladies. Capricorn women, like the men, take life very seriously, and seem to believe even one's love life takes a lot of hard work. That life is real, sibling-sign Aquarius will never deny; what Aquarius knows better than Capricorn, however, is that there's a big wonderful world out there. Capricorn women should take the time to cultivate some interesting interests outside the home or office.

Aquarius: *Polarity, Pisces:*
Masculine Air   *Feminine Water*

The Male: Theoretically, Aquarius should be a very communicative sign, belonging as it does to the air element. However, one problem with Aquarians in general and male Aquarians in particular is that they will communicate about everything in the world except their own feelings. Sometimes one wonders if they really have them. They do, of course, but dealing with emotion is something bordering on frightening for the male Aquarian. "Sob sister" Pisces may go overboard in the other direction, but provides a useful model for the Aquarian man who has trouble finding his feelings.

The Female: As youngsters, Aquarian girls usually have no lack of playmates. Later on, however, they may begin to feel left out—especially by men. No matter how charming, lively, sparkling, and/or witty she is, the female Aquarian may have few intimates. The hurly-burly of close emotional ties, with men or women, she leaves to others—like her Pisces sister. By studying a Pisces the Aquarian female can observe the receptive feminine nature at its deepest, and learn to project warmth and sympathy herself.

Pisces:	*Polarity, Aries:*
Feminine Water	*Masculine Fire*

The Male: It is sad but true that many Piscean males drift through life with little apparent direction. This in part derives from the fact that it is the most feminine of the feminine signs, in the sense of lacking self-assertion. Though you may be able to point to exceptions, it is generally true that male Pisceans are "receivers" rather than "transmitters." In boisterous, energetic Aries lies Pisces' salvation. The first sign of the zodiac is virtually antithetical to the last, and though Aries may jar Pisces' nerves, Pisces would do well to take a leaf from Aries' book.

The Female: In general, Pisces females fare better than the men of this sign. That is, however, if they stick to pretty traditional female roles. In fact, if the Piscean woman gives in to her ultranegative polarity, she can be the classic clinging vine. There is generally a great deal of creativity, but it needs focusing. Some Piscean females focus too much on creating babies. Their older-sibling sign Aries provides the perfect role model by being direct, outgoing, and "courageous" in the sense of meeting life head on.

4. WHICH HOUSE IS YOUR HOME?

A horoscope or natal map looks like a pie divided into twelve sections, or a wheel with twelve spokes. The sections are called "houses" and the spokes that divide them are called "cusps." Since the wheel makes a complete turn every twenty-four hours (actually, the daily rotation of the earth), the positions of the planets between the spokes change. The total meaning of your horoscope is therefore tremendously affected by which planets are in which houses at the moment of your birth. The astrologer views your natal map, or picture of the sky, as a freeze frame in a film. It represents one particular moment in the continuing drama of time: your moment.

That is why it is important to know your time of birth as closely as possible. Family records, your birth certificate, and the Bureau of Vital Statistics in your state are all sources you can try. For the purposes of this chapter, if you know the two-hour period within the twenty-four-hour day in which you were born, you can determine which house the sun was in at the moment of your birth, and hence which house is your "home."

Each house of the horoscope represents a different facet of the total human experience. Put another way, each house of the horoscope is a "slice of life," and the twelve slices add up to all there is for us here on earth. If you keep in mind that your sun sign is the real "you" and the sun is your "essence," you can appreciate the fact that the house that contains your sun has the greatest importance in the direction of your life.

The house of your sun sign is your "home" because it indicates the particular area of human experience in which you will play out your role this lifetime.

In the interlocking pattern of symbols that is astrology, each horoscope house corresponds to a zodiac sign and a planet. If you remember the metaphor used in an earlier chapter, the planet (in this case the sun) is the actor, the sign is the costume and makeup he wears, and the house is the particular stage set in which the action takes place. Each house also has a polarity or sex, just as the signs do. The planets, signs, and houses line up as follows:

Planet	Sign	House	Polarity
Mars	Aries	First	Positive/masculine
Venus	Taurus	Second	Negative/feminine
Mercury	Gemini	Third	Positive/masculine
Moon	Cancer	Fourth	Negative/feminine
Sun	Leo	Fifth	Positive/masculine
Mercury	Virgo	Sixth	Negative/feminine
Venus	Libra	Seventh	Positive/masculine
Pluto	Scorpio	Eighth	Negative/feminine
Jupiter	Sagittarius	Ninth	Positive/masculine
Saturn	Capricorn	Tenth	Negative/feminine
Uranus	Aquarius	Eleventh	Positive/masculine
Neptune	Pisces	Twelfth	Negative/feminine

Another general way of classifying the houses is as follows:

- Houses one, five, and nine: "personal" houses
- Houses two, six, and ten: "practical" houses
- Houses three, seven, and eleven: "social" houses

- Houses four, eight, and twelve: "unconscious" or "subconscious" houses

You might notice that these house classifications also roughly correspond to the elements, fire, earth, air, and water; that too is no accident.

The fact that your sun probably falls into a different house than the one that corresponds to your sun sign does not mean that you "become" that sign. Rather your house "colors" your life, and the way you live out your sun sign. For instance, if your sun sign is Taurus and your sun falls into the ninth house, the house of Sagittarius, it can mean that you will be the kind of Taurean personality who tends to live life on a broader and deeper level than the "pure" Taurean might.

Important! In looking for the house that corresponds to the two-hour period during which you were born, remember to take daylight saving time into account. If you have any doubts about whether or not daylight saving was in effect when you were born, a quick call to a community or state office will settle the matter.

Born between 4 and 6 a.m.—SUN IN THE FIRST HOUSE

Predawn-to-dawn births are fairly common, so many people may find that the first house is their home. Not a bad place for the sun to reside, all things considered. It is the house of *self*, and no matter what your sun sign may be, this placement lends you the opportunity to express your individuality in a positive way. In fact, "negative" or self-repressive signs may end up in the spotlight in spite of themselves with the sun placed here. Because the natural ruler of the first house is Mars, there is a kind of jet propulsion experienced here—and for some it may be uncomfortable. For others, it may be all too compatible with their natural bent.

The fire signs particularly should beware of a tendency to arrogance when the sun falls into the first house. The fiery sun further ignited by fiery Mars can create overkill in terms of the individual's sense of self. More literally, a fire sun in a fire house is a dangerous combination; most accidents are caused by impatience and impetuosity.

In general, people with the sun in the first house have a fairly clear self-image, at least once youth is past. That image may be "good" or it may be "bad"; the point is that first-house-sun people are *aware* of themselves and the personalities they project. Since respect and recognition are first-house goals, the first-house-sun person will at least try to present himself or herself in a way that is acceptable to others—or that attains his or her ends. Regardless of your sun sign, if the first house is your "home" you will experience a "cosmic itch" to be out front. A first-house sun doesn't guarantee that you will get anywhere, but it does mean you won't fail for lack of interest.

Born between 2 and 4 a.m.—SUN IN THE SECOND HOUSE

If the first-house-sun individual wants recognition, the second-house-sun person wants something far more tangible. This is the house of material possessions and security, in all senses of the word. Even a "flaky" horoscope is strengthened by a second-house sun, which places the individual in the earning/gaining/owning area of human experience. The life work may literally be banking, finance, or commodities; at any rate the life goals are likely to be sustenance and substance. Part of the effect of having the sun in the second house is to want things very badly—and to have the persistence to pursue them and get what you want. In the case of the second-house-sun person it is virtually assured, if the sun sign is reasonably strong.

As one can imagine, the earth signs and to some extent the water signs feel most "at home" in this house. The solid parameters of the second house mesh quite well with their instincts to build, preserve, and hold on. For some—particularly Taurus and Capricorn—a second-house sun may lead to an excessive desire for and concern with the material. For the fire signs, who tend to rush forward with little regard for the material consequences, a second-house sun can be a godsend, and the ticket to fortune if not fame. Fire possesses the ideas, the foresight, and the enthusiasm to succeed; the second house acts both as a much-needed "brake" and as a practical foundation. If the second house sounds a bit dull, it is. People with sun in the second house, regardless of sun sign, would do well to make an effort to broaden their horizons and look beyond merely the here and now.

Born between midnight and 2 a.m.—SUN IN THE THIRD HOUSE

Coming as it does in the first quarter of the wheel of the horoscope, the third house represents our early environment and the first relationships we form. It is sometimes called the house of brothers and sisters. What that means for the third-house-sun person is a desire to communicate, teach, and learn in a fairly basic way—the way we learned from and taught our siblings. In the world of work, many third-house-sun people may play out their career roles as schoolteachers, and writers of news, light prose, and humor.

The third house is also called the house of short journeys. In the life of the individual this often works out as a concern with what is nearby and immediate rather than what is way out there. Third-house-sun people put a high priority on their environment in terms of the kinds of people they want around them. It is a highly congenial house, coming as it does under the rulership of Mercury and Gemini. Sociability will be "forced" on the third-house-sun person who would really rather be reclusive. Even a relatively noncommunicative sign like Scorpio will "lighten up" and breathe fresher air in the third house. The third is also called one of the "mental" houses, and this should be a cautionary note for the air signs, Gemini, Libra and Aquarius. "Cool" and logical by nature, they can be positively chilly in this house; feelings should be cultivated. For all signs, going, coming, talking, writing, communicating, and socializing are the worldly things this house represents. It is in every way a "positive" house for the sun, because it puts us in direct contact with our fellow creatures, and in general smooths our contacts with them.

Born between 10 p.m. and midnight—SUN IN THE FOURTH HOUSE

The first, fourth, and tenth houses of the horoscope are particularly strong placements for the sun, and you find the sun there in many achieving horoscopes. For the fourth-house-sun person, worldly achievement may not always come easily, however, for this house is at the very bottom of the horoscope, and it takes effort to break out of it into the upper or outer reaches of life. The fourth house represents our parental home, the "nest" where our most ingrained and subconscious habits were formed. The fourth house is a comfortable place, and one can desire to stay there forever. It is a bit like the womb, and for some people, leaving it is as traumatic as birth. This is particularly true for the water signs, and to some extent for the earth signs. Their natural inertia and in some cases fear can make them cling and want to "stay home" forever. That, however, is the neurotic reaction, and most normal people with fourth-house suns do indeed enter the world—and sometimes compensate by their choice of role or profession. For instance, the fourth-house-sun woman can be the perfect stay-at-home homemaker and mother. Some signs choose the "helping" professions, such as nursing, therapy, or counseling, and thereby act out their desire to be mothered by mothering.

Whatever the sun sign, it will color the person especially vividly when the sun falls into the fourth house. There is tremendous energy here, though of a subterranean nature. It can catapult the fire signs to positions of great power and authority, though they may never feel fully comfortable with their "exposed" condition. For fourth-house-sun people the desire to retreat will always be strong.

Born between 8 and 10 p.m.—SUN IN THE FIFTH HOUSE

The keynote for the fifth house is self-expression. It differs from the first house in that the desire to make an individual statement is even stronger here—and the likelihood of making it is even greater. The fifth house—the "natural" house of Leo—can almost literally be called a stage, and an astonishing number of performers have sun in the fifth. The stamp of individuality can be put on many things by fifth-house-sun people—books, paintings, newsworthy feats, even scandalous behavior. For many people, what they "create" that bears their stamp is children. The fifth house is a wonderful placement for parents, as long as their sun sign contains the qualities of warmth and emotion. Early-education teachers are often fifth-house-sun people, and the nursery or classroom becomes their "stage."

Like the first house, the fifth sometimes forces negative signs to take a chance on life and show their natural colors publicly. Life is a gamble for anyone, but fifth-house-sun people often find that fact positively enjoyable. Literal gambling for some can become an addiction. More amorous types with fifth-house suns work out their speculative fever by taking a chance on love—often. The fifth is often called the house of romance and love affairs (as opposed to marriage, which is the province of the seventh house). The pleasure principle is a strong component of fifth-house activity, and an aspect of it that certain self-indulgent types should take seriously. There is a light note to everything connected with the fifth house, and that is not a derogatory statement. Life should be pleasurable no matter what route we follow. If all parents could learn to "play" as fifth-house-sun people do, most children would be a lot better off. The real "danger" of the fifth house is self-glorification, and fire signs particularly should watch out for this tendency.

Born between 6 and 8 p.m.—SUN IN THE SIXTH HOUSE

By contrast with the fifth house, the sixth strikes a somewhat somber note: It is the house of duty, responsibility, and service. The natural house of Virgo, the sixth house is the natural arena of "number two" people or those in backup positions. For the earth signs particularly, the sixth house is a comfortable place to hide—and there is surely nothing wrong with a life of service and dedication to a job, a person, or an idea. The problem for the earth-sign person particularly is that without some "grace notes" in his or her horoscope, all work and no play can mean a rather dull existence. There is a theory, according to the law of karma, that the sixth house is where we "pay for" the possible excesses of the fifth.

A more positive manifestation of the sixth house is efficiency. Sixth-house-sun people often have a built-in necessity to make things, people, and families work—and work well. The word "necessity" is the key, however, and many sixth-house-sun people may feel they are constantly pushing the proverbial rock uphill. This can be particularly true of the fire and air signs, who both want freedom of movement. The sixth house to some of them can seem like a "prison"; but their efforts to break out can often bear interesting and fruitful results. The fire sign in an earth house can be a dynamo of activity and production.

When disheartened, a sixth-house-sun person can feel drained, both physically and mentally. It is also known as the house of health, and a concern for the physical body can lead to hypochondria if allowed to run wild. On the positive side, sixth-house-sun people can have such a great interest in health and nutrition that it provides a life's work. Many nutritionists, physical therapists, lab researchers, and pharmacists have sixth-house suns. Some sixth-house-sun people serve so well in their chosen roles that they are singled out for commendation and/or promotion—and are less than comfortable with the attention.

Born between 4 and 6 p.m.—SUN IN THE SEVENTH HOUSE

The seventh house is exactly 180 degrees away from the first house, so, as the keynote for the first is "I," the keynote for the seventh is "we." This is the house of partnership and shared experience. In terms of totality of the horoscope, it is this house where we must "learn" that there are other people in the world. For many seventh-house-sun people this is a "given"; the concept is not difficult to deal with at all, and they are perfectly comfortable knowing they are one-half of a perfect whole. This is particularly true of the air signs, who see the logic of the situation and "know" that it is both desirable and productive to have a partner in many aspects of life. Whatever is good for one is even better for two, reasons the air sign. Even "distant" Aquarius, who may not necessarily marry, will always hook up with a group or an ideal that complements him.

Obviously, then, the "loner" signs like Aries and Scorpio are going to be unhappy in the seventh house. Since it is the house of marriage, the seventh house can be an uncomfortable home for those who want to rule the roost, regardless of sun sign. Indeed, the placement of the sun in the seventh house is often an indication of a "stronger" partner. For leaners, this is ideal; for leaders, it can spell trouble. Acceptance is the answer, for both parties to the seventh-house-sun relationship. The seventh house starts the "upper half" of the horoscope, which represents the real world, and that we are not alone in that world is an incontrovertible fact of life. Seventh-house-sun people can be superb in business and the professions, as employers, employees, and peers.

Born between 2 and 4 p.m.—SUN IN THE EIGHTH HOUSE

The house of "death and transformation" is a pretty heavy handle, but the eighth house is actually a rather good placement for the sun. The rulership of Pluto lends depth and power to this house, and though its "inhabitants" may have to share with others, they often benefit from them. Legacies and inheritances are connected with this house, and though you may never actually receive one, the practical application is that you might find your life's work in handling other people's money—a job you would do well.

"Other people's resources" is one of the taglines of this house, and "resources" means more things than money. Deep-looking eighth-house-sun people may show great acumen in psychoanalytic and/or therapeutic work. The "death and transformation" part takes earthly form in the fact that eighth-house-sun people can deal with "endings" in a positive way, sometimes turning what might be discarded into something of value. Cases in point: Undertakers and waste-disposal firms come under eighth-house rulership. More common eighth-house "endings" are the transition from childhood to parenthood and the single state to marriage.

What characterizes the eighth-house-sun person is deep commitment. Each stage or station of life is taken with great seriousness and ceremony, and there is a high degree of dedication. What this means is that an eighth-house placement can add needed depth to the "lighter" sun signs. Conversely, it can make the more freedom-loving signs feel claustrophobic. In a sense, one might call the eighth the house of "true responsibility," and as such it can be a bit oppressive.

Born between noon and 2 p.m.—SUN IN THE NINTH HOUSE

Falling under the rulership of Jupiter and Sagittarius, the ninth house is both broad and long, metaphorically speaking. It is the house of understanding, higher education, publishing, and long-distance travel. People with sun in the ninth may literally teach at college level, write, delve into philosophy and metaphysics, or work in foreign countries; or they may also simply take symbolic journeys into the far and wide. There is an expansiveness to the ninth house that is good for almost any sun sign; though for some, like Pisces, there may just be too much room to move around in and consequently they may find it harder to find a direction. For the most part, however, ninth-house-sun people feel a kind of internal freedom; they have the sense that boundaries are to be leaped over, and that they can do it—if only mentally.

Idealism and religious fervor are part of the ninth-house scene. In the great majority of people this will act as pure background to their lives in the here and now—although the desire to uplift others is often present in ninth-house-sun people. And of course, the danger of being preachy is always present as well. Fire signs are the most compatible with this house and water signs the least. Since it is the house of higher thought and the air signs are mental, they are fairly comfortable in the ninth as well. In fact, an air sign with the sun in the ninth house is the perfect combination for someone who wants to go into publishing. In sum, the ninth house is the place you will find many of the broad-minded people in this world.

Born between 10 a.m. and noon—SUN IN THE TENTH HOUSE

Along with the first and the fourth, this is one of the true "power" houses of the zodiac. It stands at the very top or zenith of the horoscope, and in astrological tradition kings and other "supermen" have sun in the tenth house. It is, in fact, uncanny how many people born near noon do achieve fame—or notoriety.

The tenth house is like the tip of the iceberg, that part the rest of the world sees. It is the house of prestige, or lack of it, because it is here in the symbolic round of the horoscope that one confronts the outer world. The tenth house stands for one's calling or vocation, and one's success or failure in it.

For some people, to be born with the sun in the tenth house is a mixed blessing. The potential of this house is so great it is hard for anyone to live up to it, and those with the sun in the tenth house will feel driven to achieve. Without a good, solid foundation in the rest of the horoscope, it is easy to come a cropper.

The tenth house comes under the rulership of Saturn and Capricorn, both stern taskmasters. The sun sign who feels Saturn pushing him forward must be prepared to work hard, take life seriously, and keep his eye on the material ball. In some horoscopes, this is an onerous destiny, and failure is likely to come simply through lack of heart.

The earth signs all do well in the tenth house, though Virgo and to some extent Taurus may not like the public aspect of it. The water signs, especially Scorpio, may be "dangerous" in the tenth house, wreaking emotional havoc by virtue of the power the tenth house confers on them. For the fire signs, it can be an unbeatable placement—the ideal house for the fiery Aries, Leo, or Sagittarius sun to shine. Air in the tenth is generally neutral, though Gemini might find it a hardship.

Born between 8 and 10 a.m.—SUN IN THE ELEVENTH HOUSE

Like the third and the seventh, the eleventh is one of the so-called "social" houses. The eleventh, which is near the end of the zodiac and therefore more "mature," is social in the broadest sense. It is here we find "friendship"—the awareness of our need for true, binding relationships—among human beings. Many people with the sun in the eleventh house do find that their happiness and success come through friendships, or at least through the willingness to reach out to all.

For certain sun signs, the eleventh house is the ideal "therapy," as it tends to wash away excess egotism and overly material objectives. The "leadership" signs may find their life work within organizations devoted to social causes or philanthropy.

The second and related meaning of the eleventh house is "hopes and wishes." Fanciful-sounding as it seems, this aspect of the eleventh is a great boon to the sun sign that falls into that house. It lends a touch of idealism to the most cynical personality, and a touch of hope to the most downtrodden horoscope. In overall "airy" horoscopes, however, it may make for a tendency to think too much and act too little. Utopia may seem like a real possibility to such a personality, and the whole life may be spent in "hoping" to find it.

Some eleventh-house-sun people seem to have been born under the proverbial "lucky star," benefiting through things that do not seem to benefit other people. There is a touch of Cinderella story in some eleventh-house-sun lives, and the possible reason is that they get back what they give out—love and friendship to all. As with Aquarius, however, eleventh-house-sun people may find their closest relationships are not as close as those of other people. The result of being friend to all also may mean belonging to no one.

Born between 6 and 8 a.m.—SUN IN THE TWELFTH HOUSE

The twelfth is the most "sub" of the subconscious houses, the deepest and darkest of all. For some sun signs, it is the ideal "hiding place"; for others, it is the worst form of solitary confinement. Into the first category fall the introspective water signs. For Cancer, Scorpio, or Pisces, having the sun in this house can literally mean one is a mystic or a contemplative. At the very least, one is extraordinarily sensitive and perceptive. For the earth signs as well as the water signs, the twelfth house—hidden away as it is—is a fairly comfortable place to be, though achievement-oriented Capricorn may suffer. It is the air and especially the fire signs who can feel unduly restrained by the placement of the sun here. Think of it as dropping a burning match into a deep, dark well.

The ancients had little good to say about the twelfth house, and though modern astrologers interpret it quite differently, they too will agree that for the twelfth-house-sun person the real world is not always a bright and cheery place to be. The inner world, and everything that implies, is the province of the twelfth house. Properly understood and integrated into one's life, a twelfth-house placement of the sun can lead to great self-understanding, and an ability to help others understand themselves. Poetry is very "twelfth-house," as is hospital work and work with those who are forced to withdraw from the world, if only temporarily. Coming under the rulership of Pisces and Neptune, the twelfth house presents a problem, but one that is not insoluble. Clarity of thought and a realistic attitude can be cultivated, and the mists of Neptune can be driven away.

5. SUN SIGN CHANGES, 1910–1975

If you were born "on the cusp" (very near the end or the beginning of a sign) you can find out what your sign really is by using the chart that follows. Many people do not realize that the sun does not "change signs" on the same day every year—or, for that matter, at the same time. For this reason the chart of sun sign changes is calculated to the minute.

How to Use the Chart

Locate your year of birth, then the month in which you were born. Let's say you were born in April of 1942. In the box for that month and year you will see

20—Tau
12:30 p.m.

That means if you were born *after* 12:30 p.m. on April 20 in 1942, you are a Taurus. If you were born before that date and time, your sun sign is the preceding one, Aries.

In this chart (as well as in the rising-sign chart) the signs are abbreviated as follows:

```
Ar  = Aries
Tau = Taurus
Gem = Gemini
Can = Cancer
Leo = Leo
Vir = Virgo
Lib = Libra
Sc  = Scorpio
Sag = Sagittarius
Cap = Capricorn
Aq  = Aquarius
Pis = Pisces
```

Note: All times given in the sun sign changes chart are
Eastern Standard. You must correct for daylight savings time (subtract one hour) and for time zone. For Central Standard Time subtract one hour; for Mountain Standard Time subtract two hours; for Pacific Standard Time subtract three hours.

	1910	1911	1912	1913	1914	1915	1916	1917	1918	1919
Jan	20–Aq 4:59 pm	20–Aq 10:52 pm	20–Aq 4:29 am	20–Aq 10:19 am	20–Aq 4:12 pm	20–Aq 10:00 pm	21–Aq 3:54 am	20–Aq 9:37 am	20–Aq 3:42 pm	19–Aq 10:21 pm
Feb	19–Pis 7:28 am	19–Pis 1:21 pm	19–Pis 6:56 pm	19–Pis 12:45 am	19–Pis 6:38 am	19–Pis 12:23 pm	19–Pis 6:18 pm	19–Pis 12:05 am	19–Pis 5:53 am	19–Pis 11:45 am
Mar	21–Ar 7:03 am	21–Ar 12:55 pm	20–Ar 6:29 pm	21–Ar 12:18 am	21–Ar 6:11 am	21–Ar 11:51 am	20–Ar 7:47 pm	20–Ar 11:37 pm	21–Ar 5:26 am	21–Ar 11:19 am
Apr	20–Tau 6:46 pm	21–Tau 12:36 am	20–Tau 6:12 am	20–Tau 12:03 pm	20–Tau 5:45 pm	20–Tau 11:28 pm	20–Tau 5:25 am	20–Tau 11:17 am	20–Tau 5:06 pm	20–Tau 10:59 pm
May	21–Gem 6:30 pm	22–Gem 12:19 am	21–Gem 5:27 am	21–Gem 11:50 am	21–Gem 5:38 pm	21–Gem 11:10 pm	21–Gem 5:06 am	21–Gem 10:59 am	21–Gem 4:46 pm	21–Gem 10:39 pm
June	22–Can 2:49 am	22–Can 8:09 am	21–Can 2:27 pm	21–Can 8:09 pm	22–Can 1:55 am	22–Can 7:29 am	21–Can 1:25 pm	21–Can 7:15 pm	22–Can 1:00 am	22–Can 6:45 am
July	23–Leo 1:43 pm	23–Leo 7:29 pm	23–Leo 7:04 pm	23–Leo 7:04 am	23–Leo 1:00 pm	23–Leo 6:49 pm	23–Leo 12:38 am	23–Leo 7:15 pm	23–Leo 12:16 pm	24–Leo 6:05 pm
Aug	23–Vir 8:27 pm	24–Vir 2:13 am	23–Vir 1:48 pm	23–Vir 1:48 pm	23–Vir 7:35 pm	24–Vir 1:16 am	23–Vir 7:09 am	23–Vir 12:54 pm	23–Vir 6:37 pm	24–Vir 12:28 am
Sept	23–Lib 5:30 pm	23–Lib 11:17 pm	23–Lib 5:08 am	23–Lib 10:53 am	23–Lib 5:35 am	23–Lib 10:24 pm	23–Lib 4:15 am	23–Lib 10:00 am	23–Lib 3:45 pm	23–Lib 9:35 pm
Oct	24–Sc 2:11 am	24–Sc 7:59 am	23–Sc 1:50 am	23–Sc 7:35 am	24–Sc 1:18 pm	24–Sc 7:10 pm	23–Sc 12:58 am	23–Sc 6:44 am	24–Sc 12:33 pm	24–Sc 6:21 pm
Nov	22–Sag 11:11 am	23–Sag 4:57 am	22–Sag 10:48 pm	22–Sag 4:36 pm	22–Sag 10:21 pm	23–Sag 3:25 am	21–Sag 9:58 am	22–Sag 3:45 pm	22–Sag 2:38 pm	23–Sag 3:25 am
Dec	22–Cap 12:12 pm	22–Cap 5:53 pm	21–Cap 11:45 pm	22–Cap 5:45 am	22–Cap 11:24 am	22–Cap 5:16 pm	21–Cap 11:45 pm	21–Cap 4:46 am	22–Cap 11:42 am	22–Cap 4:27 pm

	1920	1921	1922	1923	1924	1925	1926	1927	1928	1929
Jan	21-Aq 4:05 am	20-Aq 8:55 am	20-Aq 2:48 pm	20-Aq 8:35 pm	21-Aq 2:29 am	20-Aq 8:20 am	20-Aq 2:13 pm	20-Aq 8:12 pm	21-Aq 1:57 am	20-Aq 7:42 am
Feb	19-Pis 5:29 pm	18-Pis 11:21 pm	19-Pis 5:16 am	19-Pis 11:00 am	19-Pis 4:51 pm	18-Pis 11:43 pm	18-Pis 4:35 am	19-Pis 10:35 am	19-Pis 4:20 pm	18-Pis 10:07 pm
Mar	20-Ar 5:00 pm	20-Ar 10:51 pm	21-Ar 4:49 am	21-Ar 10:29 am	20-Ar 4:20 pm	20-Ar 11:13 am	21-Ar 4:01 am	21-Ar 11:59 am	20-Ar 3:44 pm	20-Ar 9:35 pm
Apr	20-Tau 4:39 am	20-Tau 10:32 am	20-Tau 4:29 am	20-Tau 10:06 pm	20-Tau 3:59 am	20-Tau 10:51 pm	20-Tau 3:36 pm	20-Tau 11:32 pm	20-Tau 3:17 am	20-Tau 9:11 am
May	21-Gem 4:22 am	21-Gem 10:17 am	21-Gem 9:11 pm	22-Gem 9:45 pm	21-Gem 3:41 am	21-Gem 10:33 am	21-Gem 3:15 pm	21-Gem 9:32 pm	21-Gem 2:53 am	21-Gem 8:48 am
June	21-Can 12:40 pm	21-Can 6:36 pm	22-Can 12:27 am	22-Can 6:03 am	21-Can 12:noon	21-Can 5:50 pm	21-Can 11:21 pm	22-Can 9:08 pm	21-Can 11:07 am	21-Can 5:01 pm
July	22-Leo 11:40 pm	23-Leo 5:31 am	23-Leo 11:20 am	23-Leo 5:01 pm	22-Leo 11:58 pm	23-Leo 4:45 am	23-Leo 10:25 am	23-Leo 4:17 am	22-Leo 11:02 pm	23-Leo 3:54 am
Aug	23-Vir 6:22 am	23-Vir 12:15 pm	⟨23-Vir 6:04 pm⟩	23-Vir 11:52 pm	23-Vir 5:48 am	23-Vir 11:33 am	23-Vir 5:14 pm	23-Vir 11:06 am	23-Vir 4:53 am	23-Vir 10:41 am
Sept	23-Lib 3:25 am	23-Lib 11:20 am	23-Lib 5:10 pm	23-Lib 9:04 pm	23-Lib 2:58 am	23-Lib 8:43 am	23-Lib 2:25 pm	23-Lib 8:17 am	23-Lib 2:36 am	23-Lib 7:52 am
Oct	23-Sc 12:31 pm	23-Sc 6:03 pm	23-Sc 11:53 pm	24-Sc 5:51 am	23-Sc 11:44 am	23-Sc 5:31 pm	23-Sc 11:18 pm	24-Sc 5:07 pm	23-Sc 10:55 am	23-Sc 4:41 pm
Nov	22-Sag 9:15 am	22-Sag 3:21 pm	22-Sag 8:55 pm	23-Sag 2:54 am	22-Sag 8:46 am	22-Sag 2:36 pm	22-Sag 8:28 pm	23-Sag 2:14 pm	22-Sag 8:00 am	22-Sag 1:48 am
Dec	21-Cap 10:17 pm	22-Cap 4:08 am	22-Cap 9:57 pm	22-Cap 3:53 pm	21-Cap 10:45 pm	22-Cap 3:37 am	22-Cap 9:34 pm	22-cap 3:18 pm	21-Cap 9:04 pm	23-Cap 2:53 am

(The Aug 1922 entry "23-Vir 6:04 pm" is circled on the page.)

	1930	1931	1932	1933	1934	1935	1936	1937	1938	1939
Jan	20–Aq 1:33 pm	21–Aq 7:18 pm	20–Aq 1:07 am	20–Aq 6:53 am	20–Aq 10:37 am	20–Aq 6:29 pm	21–Aq 12:12am	20–Aq 6:01 am	20–Aq 11:59 am	20–Aq 5:51 pm
Feb	19–Pis 4:00 am	19–Pis 9:06 am	19–Pis 3:29 pm	19–Pis 9:16 pm	19–Pis 3:02 am	19–Pis 8:52 am	19–Pis 2:33 pm	18–Pis 3:21 pm	19–Pis 2:20 pm	19–Pis 8:10 pm
Mar	21–Ar 3:30 am	21–Ar 9:40 am	20–Ar 2:54 pm	21–Ar 8:43 pm	21–Ar 2:28 am	21–Ar 8:19 am	20–Ar 1:58 pm	20–Ar 7:45 pm	21–Ar 1:43 am	21–Ar 7:29 am
Apr	20–Tau 3:06 pm	20–Tau 8:40 pm	20–Tau 2:28 am	20–Tau 8:19 am	20–Tau 2:00 pm	20–Tau 7:50 pm	20–Tau 1:31 am	20–Tau 7:20 am	20–Tau 1:15 pm	20–Tau 6:55 pm
May	21–Gem 2:42 pm	21–Gem 8:15 pm	21–Gem 2:07 am	21–Gem 7:57 am	21–Gem 1:35 pm	21–Gem 7:25 pm	21–Gem 1:08 am	21–Gem 6:57 am	21–Gem 12:51 pm	21–Gem 6:27 pm
June	21–Can 11:53 pm	23–Can 4:28 am	21–Can 10:23 am	21–Can 4:12 pm	21–Can 9:48 pm	22–Can 3:32 am	21–Can 9:22 am	21–Can 3:12 pm	21–Can 9:04 pm	22–Can 2:40 am
July	23–Leo 10:42 am	23–Leo 3:21 pm	22–Leo 9:18 pm	23–Leo 3:06 am	23–Leo 8:42 am	23–Leo 2:33 pm	22–Leo 8:18 pm	23–Leo 2:07 am	23–Leo 7:57 am	23–Leo 1:37 pm
Aug	23–Vir 4:27 pm	23–Vir 10:10 pm	23–Vir 4:06 am	23–Vir 9:53 am	23–Vir 3:32 pm	23–Vir 9:24 pm	23–Vir 3:11 am	23–Vir 8:58 am	23–Vir 2:46 pm	23–Vir 8:31 pm
Sept	23–Lib 1:35 pm	23–Lib 7:23 pm	23–Lib 1:16 am	23–Lib 7:01 am	23–Lib 10:45 am	23–Lib 6:38 pm	23–Lib 12:26 am	23–Lib 6:13 am	23–Lib 12:noon	23–Lib 5:50 pm
Oct	23–Sc 11:25 pm	24–Sc 4:15 pm	23–Sc 10:04 am	23–Sc 3:48 pm	23–Sc 9:35 pm	24–Sc 3:29 am	23–Sc 10:18 am	23–Sc 3:06 pm	23–Sc 8:54 pm	24–Sc 2:46 pm
Nov	22–Sag 7:34 pm	23–Sag 1:25 pm	22–Sag 7:10 am	22–Sag 10:53 am	22–Sag 6:44 pm	23–Sag 12:35 am	22–Sag 6:25 pm	22–Sag 12:17 pm	22–Sag 6:06 pm	22–Sag 11:59 pm
Dec	22–Cap 8:40 am	22–Cap 2:30 pm	21–Cap 8:14 pm	22–Cap 1:58 am	22–Cap 5:49 pm	22–Cap 1:37 pm	21–Cap 7:27 pm	22–Cap 1:22 am	22–Cap 7:13 am	22–Cap 1:05 pm

	1940	1941	1942	1943	1944	1945	1946	1947	1948
Jan	20–Aq 11:44 pm	20–Aq 5:34 am	20–Aq 11:16 am	20–Aq 5:20 pm	20–Aq 11:09 pm	20–Aq 4:55 am	20–Aq 10:44 am	20–Aq 4:23 pm	20–Aq 10:18 pm
Feb	19–Pis 2:04 pm	18–Pis 7:59 pm	19–Pis 1:39 am	19–Pis 7:41 am	19–Pis 1:28 pm	18–Pis 7:15 pm	19–Pis 1:10 am	19–Pis 6:53 am	19–Pis 12:37 pm
Mar	20–Ar 1:24 pm	20–Ar 7:21 pm	21–Ar 1:03 am	21–Ar 7:03 am	21–Ar 12:49 pm	20–Ar 6:38 pm	21–Ar 12:34 pm	21–Ar 6:13 pm	20–Ar 11:57 am
Apr	20–Tau 12:51 am	20–Tau 6:51 am	20–Tau 12:30 pm	20–Tau 6:32 pm	20–Tau 12:18 am	20–Tau 6:08 am	20–Tau 12:03 pm	20–Tau 5:40 pm	19–Tau 11:25 pm
May	21–Gem 12:23 am	21–Gem 6:23 am	21–Gem 12:01 pm	21–Gem 6:03 pm	20–Gem 11:51 pm	21–Gem 5:41 am	21–Gem 1:34 am	21–Gem 5:04 pm	20–Gem 10:58 pm
June	21–Can 8:37 am	21–Can 2:33 am	21–Can 8:08 pm	22–Can 2:13 am	21–Can 9:03 am	21–Can 1:52 pm	21–Can 7:45 pm	22–Can 1:19 am	21–Can 7:11 am
July	22–Leo 7:34 pm	23–Leo 1:26 am	23–Leo 6:59 am	23–Leo 1:05 pm	22–Leo 6:55 pm	23–Leo 12:48 pm	23–Leo 6:37 am	23–Leo 12:12 pm	22–Leo 6:06 pm
Aug	23–Vir 2:21 am	23–Vir 8:30 am	23–Vir 1:50 pm	23–Vir 7:55 pm	23–Vir 1:47 am	23–Vir 7:36 am	23–Vir 1:23 pm	23–Vir 7:09 pm	23–Vir 1:03 am
Sept	22–Lib 11:46 pm	23–Lib 5:33 am	23–Lib 11:10 am	23–Lib 5:12 pm	22–Lib 11:02 pm	23–Lib 4:50 am	23–Lib 10:41 am	23–Lib 4:29 pm	22–Lib 10:22 pm
Oct	23–Sc 8:39 am	23–Sc 2:22 pm	24–Sc 8:01 pm	24–Sc 2:09 am	23–Sc 7:57 am	23–Sc 1:45 pm	23–Sc 7:37 pm	24–Sc 1:27 am	23–Sc 7:19 am
Nov	22–Sag 5:49 am	22–Sag 11:38 am	22–Sag 5:23 pm	22–Sag 11:22 pm	22–Sag 5:09 am	22–Sag 10:56 am	22–Sag 4:47 pm	22–Sag 10:38 pm	22–Sag 4:29 am
Dec	21–Cap 6:55 pm	22–Cap 12:44 pm	22–Cap 6:31 pm	22–Cap 12:30 pm	21–Cap 6:15 pm	22–Cap 12:04 am	22–Cap 5:54 pm	22–Cap 11:44 am	21–Cap 5:23 pm

	1949	1950	1951	1952	1953	1954	1955	1956	1957
Jan	20-Aq 4:11 am	20-Aq 10:00 am	20-Aq 3:53 pm	20-Aq 9:38 pm	20-Aq 3:22 am	20-Aq 9:14 am	20-Aq 3:03 pm	20-Aq 8:49 pm	20-Aq 2:43 am
Feb	18-Pis 6:27 pm	19-Pis 12:16 am	19-Pis 6:10 am	19-Pis 11:57 am	18-Pis 5:41 pm	19-Pis 11:33 pm	19-Pis 5:19 am	19-Pis 11:05 am	18-Pis 5:01 pm
Mar	20-Ar 5:49 pm	20-Ar 11:30 pm	21-Ar 5:26 am	20-Ar 11:14 am	20-Ar 5:01 pm	20-Ar 10:54 pm	21-Ar 4:36 am	20-Ar 10:21 am	20-Ar 4:17 pm
Apr	20-Tau 5:18 am	20-Tau 11:00 am	20-Tau 4:49 pm	20-Tau 10:37 pm	19-Tau 4:26 am	20-Tau 10:20 am	20-Tau 3:58 pm	19-Tau 9:44 pm	20-Tau 3:45 am
May	21-Gem 4:51 am	21-Gem 10:27 am	21-Gem 4:15 pm	20-Gem 10:04 pm	21-Gem 3:53 am	21-Gem 9:48 am	21-Gem 3:25 pm	20-Gem 9:13 pm	21-Gem 3:09 am
June	21-Can 1:03 pm	21-Can 6:37 pm	22-Can 12:25 am	21-Can 6:13 am	21-Can 12:noon	21-Can 5:55 pm	21-Can 11:32 pm	21-Can 5:24 am	21-Can 11:21 am
July	22-Leo 1:58 pm	23-Leo 5:30 am	23-Leo 11:29 am	22-Leo 5:05 pm	22-Leo 10:53 pm	23-Leo 4:45 am	23-Leo 10:25 am	22-Leo 4:20 pm	22-Leo 10:13 pm
Aug	23-Vir 6:49 pm	23-Vir 12:24 pm	23-Vir 6:22 pm	23-Vir 12:03 am	23-Vir 5:46 am	23-Vir 11:37 am	23-Vir 5:19 pm	22-Vir 11:15 pm	23-Vir 5:07 pm
Sept	23-Lib 4:05 am	23-Lib 9:44 am	23-Lib 3:38 pm	22-Lib 9:24 pm	23-Lib 3:07 am	23-Lib 8:56 am	23-Lib 2:42 pm	22-Lib 8:30 pm	23-Lib 2:27 am
Oct	23-Sc 1:04 pm	23-Sc 6:48 pm	23-Sc 12:37 am	23-Sc 6:22 am	23-Sc 12:07 pm	23-Sc 5:58 pm	22-Sc 11:44 pm	23-Sc 5:35 am	23-Sc 11:33 am
Nov	22-Sag 10:17 am	22-Sag 4:03 pm	22-Sag 9:52 pm	22-Sag 3:36 am	22-Sag 9:23 am	22-Sag 3:14 pm	22-Sag 9:02 pm	22-Sag 2:51 am	22-Sag 8:45 am
Dec	21-Cap 11:24 am	22-Cap 5:14 am	22-Cap 11:01 am	21-Cap 4:44 pm	21-Cap 10:22 pm	22-Cap 4:25 am	22-Cap 10:12 am	21-Cap 4:00 pm	21-Cap 9:49 pm

	1958	1959	1960	1961	1962	1963	1964	1965	1968
Jan	20-Aq 2:20 pm	20-Aq 2:20 pm	20-Aq 8:11 pm	20-Aq 2:02 am	20-Aq 7:49 am	20-Aq 1:55 pm	19-Aq 7:43 pm	20-Aq 1:30 am	20-Aq 8:21 am
Feb	18-Pis 10:49 pm	19-Pis 4:38 pm	19-Pis 10:26 am	18-Pis 6:27 pm	18-Pis 10:16 am	19-Pis 4:09 am	19-Pis 10:25 am	18-Pis 3:49 pm	18-Pis 9:39 pm
Mar	20-Ar 10:06 pm	21-Ar 3:55 am	20-Ar 9:43 am	20-Ar 5:27 am	20-Ar 9:30 pm	21-Ar 3:20 am	20-Ar 9:43 am	20-Ar 3:05 pm	20-Ar 8:53 pm
Apr	20-Tau 9:28 am	20-Tau 3:17 pm	20-Tau 10:06 pm	20-Tau 2:33 am	20-Tau 8:51 am	20-Tau 2:37 pm	19-Tau 9:00 pm	20-Tau 2:27 am	20-Tau 8:12 am
May	21-Gem 8:52 am	21-Gem 2:38 am	20-Gem 8:33 pm	21-Gem 1:51 am	21-Gem 8:17 am	21-Gem 1:59 pm	20-Gem 8:33 pm	21-Gem 1:27 am	21-Gem 7:33 am
June	21-Can 4:57 pm	21-Can 10:50 pm	21-Can 4:43 am	21-Can 10:12 am	21-Can 4:24 pm	21-Can 11:04 pm	21-Can 4:43 am	21-Can 9:56 am	21-Can 3:33 pm
July	23-Leo 3:51 am	23-Leo 9:45 am	22-Leo 5:38 pm	22-Leo 9:12 pm	23-Leo 3:19 am	23-Leo 9:00 am	22-Leo 3:38 pm	22-Leo 8:49 pm	23-Leo 2:24 am
Aug	23-Vir 10:47 am	23-Vir 4:44 pm	22-Vir 10:35 pm	23-Vir 3:46 am	23-Vir 10:13 am	23-Vir 3:58 pm	22-Vir 10:35 pm	23-Vir 3:43 am	23-Vir 9:18 am
Sept	23-Lib 5:10 am	23-Lib 2:09 pm	22-Lib 8:00 pm	23-Lib 1:26 am	23-Lib 7:35 am	23-Lib 1:24 pm	22-Lib 8:00 pm	23-Lib 1:06 am	23-Lib 6:43 am
Oct	23-Sc 5:12 am	23-Sc 11:12 pm	23-Sc 5:03 am	23-Sc 10:46 am	23-Sc 4:41 pm	23-Sc 11:30 pm	23-Sc 5:03 am	23-Sc 10:11 am	23-Sc 3:52 pm
Nov	22-Sag 2:30 am	22-Sag 8:23 pm	22-Sag 2:19 am	22-Sag 8:10 am	22-Sag 2:02 pm	22-Sag 7:50 pm	22-Sag 2:19 am	22-Sag 7:30 am	22-Sag 1:15 pm
Dec	22-Cap 3:40 am	22-Cap 9:35 am	21-Cap 5:27 pm	21-Cap 9:25 pm	22-Cap 3:15 am	22-Cap 9:02 pm	21-Cap 3:27 pm	21-Cap 8:41 pm	22-Cap 2:29 pm

	1967	1968	1969	1970	1971	1972	1973	1974	1975
Jan	20–Aq 1:05 pm	20–Aq 6:54 pm	20–Aq 12:30 am	20–Aq 6:25 am	20–Aq 12:14 pm	20–Aq 6:00 pm	19–Aq 11:49 pm	20–Aq 5:47 am	20–Aq 11:37 am
Feb	19–Pis 3:25 am	19–Pis 9:11 am	18–Pis 2:47 pm	18–Pis 8:43 pm	19–Pis 2:28 am	19–Pis 8:12am	18–Pis 2:02 pm	18–Pis 8:00 pm	19–Pis 1:51 am
Mar	21–Ar 2:37 am	20–Ar 8:22 am	20–Ar 2:08 pm	20–Ar 7:59 pm	21–Ar 1:28 am	20–Ar 7:22 am	20–Ar 1:13 pm	20–Ar 7:08 pm	21–Ar 12:58 am
Apr	20–Tau 1:56 am	19–Tau 7:42 pm	20–Tau 1:18 am	20–Tau 5:16 am	20–Tau 12:54 pm	19–Tau 6:38 pm	20–Tau 12:31 am	20–Tau 5:19 am	20–Tau 12:08 pm
May	21–Gem 1:19 pm	20–Gem 7:07 pm	21–Gem 12:41 am	21–Gem 6:32 am	21–Gem 12:16 pm	20–Gem 6:00 pm	20–Gem 11:54 pm	21–Gem 5:37 am	21–Gem 1:25 pm
June	21–Can 4:23 pm	21–Can 1:13 am	21–Can 6:55 am	21–Can 2:43 pm	21–Can 8:21 pm	21–Can 2:07 am	21–Can 8:01 am	21–Can 1:38 pm	21–Can 7:27 pm
July	23–Leo 8:16 am	22–Leo 2:13 pm	22–Leo 8:05 pm	23–Leo 1:38 am	23–Leo 7:15 am	22–Leo 1:03 pm	22–Leo 6:56 pm	23–Leo 12:30 am	23–Leo 7:23 am
Aug	23–Vir 3:13 pm	22–Vir 9:52 pm	23–Vir 2:35 am	23–Vir 6:35 am	23–Vir 2:16 pm	22–Vir 8:04 pm	23–Vir 1:55 am	23–Vir 7:29 am	23–Vir 1:24 pm
Sept	23–Lib 12:38 pm	22–Lib 6:26 pm	23–Lib 12:07 am	23–Lib 5:59 am	23–Lib 11:47 am	22–Lib 5:34 pm	22–Lib 11:22 pm	23–Lib 4:59 am	23–Lib 10:56 am
Oct	23–Sc 9:44 pm	23–Sc 1:30 am	23–Sc 9:03 am	23–Sc 3:05 pm	22–Sc 8:53 pm	23–Sc 2:42 am	23–Sc 8:31 am	23–Sc 2:12 pm	23–Sc 8:07 pm
Nov	22–Sag 7:05 pm	22–Sag 12:59 am	22–Sag 6:23 am	22–Sag 12:25 pm	22–Sag 6:15 pm	22–Sag 12:04 am	22–Sag 5:55 am	22–Sag 11:39 am	22–Sag 5:32 pm
Dec	22–Cap 8:17 am	21–Cap 2:00 pm	21–Cap 7:44 pm	22–Cap 1:36 am	22–Cap 5:26 am	21–Cap 1:14 pm	21–Cap 7:09 pm	22–Cap 12:57 am	22–Cap 7:47 am

6. FIND YOUR RISING SIGN

It is easier than many people think to find out your rising sign. One reason is that it is based on "universal" or "sidereal" time—the measure used in space travel. To ascertain your rising sign, look through the following chart and locate the birthdate nearest your birth date; look across and locate the time nearest your birth time. Remember that if daylight saving time was in effect at your birth, you must subtract one hour from the time stated on your birth certificate. In the section for your date and time, you will find an abbreviation for the sign that was rising when you were born. For instance, if your birthdate is June 12 at 9:30 a.m., your rising sign is Leo; if you were born on the same date at 9:30 p.m., your rising sign is Capricorn.

You will notice that the *year* you were born does not affect your rising sign. However, the geographical latitude does. These tables are calculated for the middle latitudes of the United States. If you were born far to the south, it is wise to look at the sign that *follows* your rising sign as well. If you were born far to the north, check out the *previous* sign.

	1 AM	2 AM	3 AM	4 AM	5 AM	6 AM	7 AM	8 AM	9 AM	10 AM	11 AM	12 NOON
Jan 1	Lib	Sc	Sc	Sc	Sag	Sag	Cap	Cap	Aq	Aq	Pis	Ar
Jan 9	Lib	Sc	Sc	Sag	Sag	Sag	Cap	Cap	Aq	Pis	Ar	Tau
Jan 17	Sc	Sc	Sc	Sag	Sag	Cap	Cap	Aq	Aq	Pis	Ar	Tau
Jan 25	Sc	Sc	Sag	Sag	Sag	Cap	Cap	Aq	Pis	Ar	Tau	Tau
Feb 2	Sc	Sc	Sag	Sag	Cap	Cap	Aq	Pis	Pis	Ar	Tau	Gem
Feb 10	Sc	Sag	Sag	Sag	Cap	Cap	Aq	Pis	Ar	Tau	Tau	Gem
Feb 18	Sc	Sag	Sag	Cap	Cap	Aq	Pis	Pis	Ar	Tau	Gem	Gem
Feb 26	Sag	Sag	Sag	Cap	Aq	Aq	Pis	Ar	Tau	Tau	Gem	Gem
Mar 6	Sag	Sag	Cap	Cap	Aq	Pis	Pis	Ar	Tau	Gem	Gem	Cap
Mar 14	Sag	Cap	Cap	Aq	Aq	Pis	Ar	Tau	Tau	Gem	Gem	Can
Mar 22	Sag	Cap	Cap	Aq	Pis	Ar	Ar	Tau	Gem	Gem	Can	Can
Mar 30	Cap	Cap	Aq	Pis	Pis	Ar	Tau	Tau	Gem	Can	Can	Can
Apr 7	Cap	Cap	Aq	Pis	Ar	Ar	Tau	Gem	Gem	Can	Can	Leo
Apr 14	Cap	Aq	Aq	Pis	Ar	Tau	Tau	Gem	Gem	Can	Can	Leo
Apr 22	Cap	Aq	Pis	Ar	Ar	Tau	Gem	Gem	Gem	Can	Leo	Leo
Apr 30	Aq	Aq	Pis	Ar	Tau	Tau	Gem	Can	Can	Can	Leo	Leo
May 8	Aq	Pis	Ar	Ar	Tau	Gem	Gem	Can	Can	Leo	Leo	Leo
May 16	Aq	Pis	Ar	Tau	Gem	Gem	Can	Can	Can	Leo	Leo	Vir
May 24	Pis	Ar	Ar	Tau	Gem	Gem	Can	Can	Leo	Leo	Leo	Vir
June 1	Pis	Ar	Tau	Gem	Gem	Can	Can	Can	Leo	Leo	Vir	Vir
June 9	Ar	Ar	Tau	Gem	Gem	Can	Can	Leo	Leo	Leo	Vir	Vir
June 17	Ar	Tau	Gem	Gem	Can	Can	Can	Leo	Leo	Vir	Vir	Vir
June 25	Tau	Tau	Gem	Gem	Can	Can	Leo	Leo	Leo	Vir	Vir	Lib
July 3	Tau	Gem	Gem	Can	Can	Can	Leo	Leo	Vir	Vir	Vir	Lib
July 11	Tau	Gem	Gem	Can	Can	Leo	Leo	Leo	Vir	Vir	Lib	Lib
July 18	Gem	Gem	Can	Can	Can	Leo	Leo	Vir	Vir	Vir	Lib	Lib
July 26	Gem	Gem	Can	Can	Leo	Leo	Vir	Vir	Vir	Lib	Lib	Lib
Aug 3	Gem	Can	Can	Can	Leo	Leo	Vir	Vir	Vir	Lib	Lib	Sc
Aug 11	Gem	Can	Can	Leo	Leo	Leo	Vir	Vir	Lib	Lib	Lib	Sc
Aug 18	Can	Can	Can	Leo	Leo	Vir	Vir	Vir	Lib	Lib	Sc	Sc
Aug 27	Can	Can	Leo	Leo	Leo	Vir	Vir	Vir	Lib	Lib	Sc	Sc
Sept 4	Can	Can	Leo	Leo	Leo	Vir	Vir	Vir	Lib	Lib	Sc	Sc
Sept 12	Can	Leo	Leo	Leo	Vir	Vir	Lib	Lib	Lib	Sc	Sc	Sag
Sept 30	Leo	Leo	Leo	Vir	Vir	Vir	Lib	Lib	Sc	Sc	Sc	Sag
Sept 30	Leo	Leo	Leo	Vir	Vir	Vir	Lib	Lib	Sc	Sc	Sag	Sag
Oct 6	Leo	Leo	Vir	Vir	Vir	Lib	Lib	Sc	Sc	Sc	Sag	Sag
Oct 14	Leo	Vir	Vir	Vir	Lib	Lib	Lib	Sc	Sc	Sag	Sag	Cap
Oct 22	Leo	Vir	Vir	Lib	Lib	Lib	Sc	Sc	Sc	Sag	Sag	Cap
Oct 30	Vir	Vir	Vir	Lib	Lib	Sc	Sc	Sc	Sag	Sag	Cap	Cap
Nov 7	Vir	Vir	Lib	Lib	Lib	Sc	Sc	Sc	Sag	Sag	Cap	Cap
Nov 15	Vir	Vir	Lib	Lib	Sc	Sc	Sc	Sag	Sag	Cap	Cap	Aq
Nov 23	Vir	Lib	Lib	Lib	Sc	Sc	Sag	Sag	Sag	Cap	Cap	Aq
Dec 1	Vir	Lib	Lib	Sc	Sc	Sc	Sag	Sag	Cap	Cap	Aq	Aq
Dec 9	Lib	Lib	Lib	Sc	Sc	Sag	Sag	Sag	Cap	Cap	Aq	Pis
Dec 18	Lib	Lib	Sc	Sc	Sc	Sag	Sag	Cap	Cap	Aq	Aq	Pis
Dec 28	Lib	Lib	Sc	Sc	Sag	Sag	Sag	Cap	Aq	Aq	Pis	Ar

Rising Signs—P.M. Births

	1 PM	2 PM	3 PM	4 PM	5 PM	6 PM	7 PM	8 PM	9 PM	10 PM	11 PM	12 MIDNIGHT
Jan 1	Tau	Gem	Gem	Can	Can	Can	Leo	Leo	Vir	Vir	Vir	Lib
Jan 9	Tau	Gem	Gem	Can	Can	Leo	Leo	Leo	Vir	Vir	Vir	Lib
Jan 17	Gem	Gem	Can	Can	Can	Leo	Leo	Vir	Vir	Vir	Lib	Lib
Jan 25	Gem	Gem	Can	Can	Leo	Leo	Leo	Vir	Vir	Lib	Lib	Lib
Feb 2	Gem	Can	Can	Can	Leo	Leo	Vir	Vir	Vir	Lib	Lib	Sc
Feb 10	Gem	Can	Can	Leo	Leo	Leo	Vir	Vir	Lib	Lib	Lib	Sc
Feb 18	Can	Can	Can	Leo	Leo	Vir	Vir	Vir	Lib	Lib	Sc	Sc
Feb 26	Can	Can	Leo	Leo	Leo	Vir	Vir	Lib	Lib	Lib	Sc	Sc
Mar 6	Can	Leo	Leo	Leo	Vir	Vir	Vir	Lib	Lib	Sc	Sc	Sc
Mar 14	Can	Leo	Leo	Vir	Vir	Vir	Lib	Lib	Lib	Sc	Sc	Sag
Mar 22	Leo	Leo	Leo	Vir	Vir	Lib	Lib	Lib	Sc	Sc	Sc	Sag
Mar 30	Leo	Leo	Vir	Vir	Vir	Lib	Lib	Sc	Sc	Sc	Sag	Sag
Apr 7	Leo	Leo	Vir	Vir	Lib	Lib	Lib	Sc	Sc	Sc	Sag	Sag
Apr 14	Leo	Vir	Vir	Vir	Lib	Lib	Sc	Sc	Sc	Sag	Sag	Cap
Apr 22	Leo	Vir	Vir	Lib	Lib	Sc	Sc	Sc	Sag	Sag	Cap	Cap
Apr 30	Vir	Vir	Vir	Lib	Lib	Sc	Sc	Sc	Sag	Sag	Cap	Cap
May 8	Vir	Vir	Lib	Lib	Lib	Sc	Sc	Sag	Sag	Sag	Cap	Cap
May 16	Vir	Vir	Lib	Lib	Sc	Sc	Sc	Sag	Sag	Cap	Cap	Aq
May 24	Vir	Lib	Lib	Lib	Sc	Sc	Sag	Sag	Sag	Cap	Cap	Aq
June 1	Vir	Lib	Lib	Sc	Sc	Sc	Sag	Sag	Cap	Cap	Aq	Aq
June 9	Lib	Lib	Lib	Sc	Sc	Sag	Sag	Sag	Cap	Cap	Aq	Pis
June 17	Lib	Lib	Sc	Sc	Sc	Sag	Sag	Cap	Cap	Aq	Aq	Pis
June 25	Lib	Lib	Sc	Sc	Sag	Sag	Sag	Cap	Cap	Aq	Pis	Ar
July 3	Lib	Sc	Sc	Sc	Sag	Sag	Cap	Cap	Aq	Aq	Pis	Ar
July 11	Lib	Sc	Sc	Sag	Sag	Sag	Cap	Cap	Aq	Pis	Ar	Tau
July 18	Sc	Sc	Sc	Sag	Sag	Cap	Cap	Aq	Aq	Pis	Ar	Tau
July 26	Sc	Sc	Sag	Sag	Sag	Cap	Cap	Aq	Pis	Ar	Tau	Tau
Aug 3	Sc	Sc	Sag	Sag	Cap	Cap	Aq	Aq	Pis	Ar	Tau	Gem
Aug 11	Sc	Sag	Sag	Sag	Cap	Cap	Aq	Pis	Ar	Tau	Tau	Gem
Aug 18	Sc	Sag	Sag	Cap	Cap	Aq	Pis	Pis	Ar	Tau	Gem	Gem
Aug 27	Sag	Sag	Sag	Cap	Cap	Aq	Pis	Ar	Tau	Tau	Gem	Gem
Sept 4	Sag	Sag	Cap	Cap	Aq	Pis	Pis	Ar	Tau	Gem	Gem	Can
Sept 12	Sag	Sag	Cap	Aq	Aq	Pis	Ar	Tau	Tau	Gem	Gem	Can
Sept 20	Sag	Cap	Cap	Aq	Pis	Pis	Ar	Tau	Gem	Gem	Can	Can
Sept 28	Cap	Cap	Aq	Aq	Pis	Ar	Tau	Tau	Gem	Gem	Can	Can
Oct 6	Cap	Cap	Aq	Pis	Ar	Ar	Tau	Gem	Gem	Can	Can	Leo
Oct 14	Cap	Aq	Aq	Pis	Ar	Tau	Tau	Gem	Gem	Can	Can	Leo
Oct 22	Cap	Aq	Pis	Ar	Ar	Tau	Gem	Gem	Can	Can	Leo	Leo
Oct 30	Aq	Aq	Pis	Ar	Tau	Tau	Gem	Can	Can	Can	Leo	Leo
Nov 7	Aq	Aq	Pis	Ar	Tau	Tau	Gem	Can	Can	Can	Leo	Leo
Nov 15	Aq	Pis	Ar	Tau	Gem	(Gem)	Can	Can	Can	Leo	Leo	Vir
Nov 23	Pis	Ar	Ar	Tau	Gem	Gem	Can	Can	Leo	Leo	Leo	Vir
Dec 1	Pis	Ar	Tau	Gem	Gem	Can	Can	Can	Leo	Leo	Vir	Vir
Dec 9	Ar	Tau	Tau	Gem	Gem	Can	Can	Can	Leo	Leo	Vir	Vir
Dec 18	Ar	Tau	Gem	Gem	Can	Can	Can	Leo	Leo	Vir	Vir	Vir
Dec 28	Tau	Tau	Gem	Gem	Can	Can	Leo	Leo	Vir	Vir	Vir	Lib

7. THE PLANETS: KEY TO COMPATIBILITY

In popular astrology there is so much emphasis on the signs of the zodiac that it is easy to forget the planets, which are in fact the prime movers of personality. In the "occult" tradition that underlies all astrological thought, the human being is seen as a microcosm of our solar system—that is, a miniature of the macrocosm of our universe. In medical astrology each part of the body is "ruled" by a different planet; in natal astrology certain personality traits are ascribed to certain planets. It is from the planets that the signs of the zodiac receive their particular individuality—which is why they are the key to interpersonal compatibility. The source of the "energy" we give off, the planets determine how that energy interacts with that of others. Some planetary combinations signal clash and conflict; others a neutralizing of energy; still others a sparky but interesting friction, or a beautiful synergy.

Which Planets Rule Which Signs?

In our solar system there are at present ten known "planets." (Astrological terminology takes the liberty of calling the sun and moon "planets" in the sense that they also rule or correspond to specific signs of the zodiac.) Since there are twelve signs of the zodiac, two planets—Mercury and Venus—rule two signs each. These are the rulership "assignments" most modern astrologers give the planets:

Sun	Leo
Moon	Cancer
Mercury	Gemini and Virgo
Venus	Taurus and Libra
Mars	Aries
Jupiter	Sagittarius
Saturn	Capricorn
Uranus	Aquarius
Neptune	Pisces
Pluto	Scorpio

People sometimes point to an apparent "flaw" in the planet-assignment system: What did astrologers do before the discovery of the "modern" planets—Uranus, Neptune, and Pluto? Early astrologers indeed knew of only seven planets, which means certain signs have both "traditional" and "modern" rulers.

	Ancient Ruler	Modern Ruler
Aquarius	Saturn	Uranus
Pisces	Jupiter	Neptune
Scorpio	Mars	Pluto

Some astrologers believe there are still planets to come, and that someday we'll have a neat twelve-planet, twelve-sign arrangement. However, planetary assignments are far from arbitrary. As a matter of fact, when looking at your own compatibility pattern in this chapter, it is wise to look at *both* your ancient and your modern ruler if you are a Scorpio, an Aquarian, or a Pisces. You probably will find "parts of yourself" in each place.

If you think about it, you realize our language is peppered with planet-derived descriptions of moods and personality types. One can be said to have a "sunny" disposition; "lunatics" were once thought to be moonstruck to the ultimate degree; you march to "martial" music; "jovial" people are often ruled by Jove, the Latin name for Jupiter; "mercurial" types move fast and are hard to pin down, like the metal itself.

Astrology has received a lot of good press in recent years in the area of planetary influences on personality. A French statistician, Michel Gaquelin, and his wife undertook a research project designed to "disprove" astrology. Instead, their research took them in a surprisingly positive direction. This scientific team now claim they have statistical proof that certain planets—when prominently placed in the horoscope—are a definite factor in the careers of many famous people. In their book, *Your Personality and the Planets*, the Gaquelins delineate the character of a number of famous individuals with respect to their dominant planet or planets. The list ranges from "Jupiterian" Franklin Delano Roosevelt to "Saturnine" Richard Nixon, and includes people like successful businessman Jean Paul Getty (Saturn), Brigitte Bardot (Venus), Mohammad Ali (Mars), George Bernard Shaw (moon), Adolph Hitler (Jupiter), and Elvis Presley (Jupiter).

While the Gaquelins based their conclusions on *only* the planets and their placement in the horoscope and *not* on the zodiac signs, for our purposes here your dominant planet will be the one that rules your sun sign. Keep in mind, however, that the total horoscope is a mixture of planetary influences. While the ruler of your sun sign is generally the most important, in some cases the planet that rules your rising sign can have a great or almost equal influence on your personality and hence on your compatibility with others. If you know the time of day you were born, use the table on pages 69 to 70 to determine your rising sign, and read those sections of this chapter as well.

The Cast of Characters

When dealing with symbolic concepts like the influence of the planets it is sometimes most productive to use the "personification" technique. In the dialogues that follow, each planet will "speak" according to its nature. Here are some clues to help you visualize the characters in these mini-dramas designed to illustrate compatibility. Like the signs, each planet has a "sex." At first you may find it confusing to think of yourself, as defined by your ruling planet, as a person of the opposite sex. Far from being a confusion, this factor has great importance in the assessment of compatibility, so it is wise to make the effort to think of yourself in a different sex role.

Sun: A prepossessing male who can exert great authority and often thinks of himself as the center of the universe. He is not particularly insightful, however, and his charm often stems from his "innocence."

Moon: A warm and sympathetic lady who sometimes overreacts because she feels all sensations and emotions so acutely—both her own and those of other people. She would take care of you if she could.

Mercury: A complex hermaphrodite with several signs as well as sides to his/her character. Clever and often witty, Mercury can be evasive, exacting, entertaining, and exasperating—sometimes all at the same time.

Venus: A lovely lady who loves the more beautiful things in this world. Peace and harmony are her true goals, and she will have them if she can—sometimes by passive force, sometimes by smiling stubbornness. A sybarite, she can surprise with her healthy desires—though she is fastidious.

Mars: A virile young man with winning on his mind. He talks tough sometimes, which can make you overlook his instinctive generosity. Impatient to a fault, he sometimes quits the field before the race is over.

Jupiter: A jovial, expansive character who sometimes acts a little like Daddy Warbucks. Capable of magnificent gestures as well as startling frankness, he is generally so good-humored that people seek his company. He hates to be alone.

Saturn: A terribly hardworking, serious fellow, he seemed old at birth. Patience, thrift, stick-to-itiveness, and punctuality can be numbered among his virtues; sadness, rigidity, and mistrust can bring both him and others down.

Uranus: A hermaphrodite with a definite slant toward the male polarity. Ingenious and sometimes even brilliant, Uranus can be quite unpredictable, and hence unsettling to more settled types. In his life there's always something new.

Neptune: A mysterious older woman who seems to know the secrets of the universe. She can charm you with her hazy, beautiful thoughts and uplift you with her idealism. The problem is: Does she have substance?

Pluto: A powerful, determined male who can be a bit of an enigma. You feel his force rather than see it, because he often wears a mask of subtle self-control. Don't mess with him, however, if you value your life and your sanity.

Each of the following sections sets up a situation which revolves around one of the planets. That planet asks a question or makes a statement to which all of the other planets must respond. Though some of the situations are social, some in the business world, and some romantic, the reactions of the "answering" planets can easily be translated to another sphere, and remain both typical and indicative of their interaction with the central planet. Venus and Mercury are given two roles each to reflect their "positive" and their "negative" sides.

1. Central Planet: The Sun

The sun has just been promoted to a position of greater authority. He talks with each of the people in his department who will be working for him—some of whom have been passed over. The sun is elated, but a little nervous. The sun asks: "How do you think it will be working together?"

Another sun: "This may come as a surprise to you, but I turned down the job. So long—I've got bigger things in mind."

Moon: "I know it will be difficult for you at first, but I will do all I can to help. Just remember, I have good days and bad days."

Mercury #1: "I'm all for it; you deserve the job. I could handle it, but I've got too many outside interests."

Mercury #2: "I hope you'll let me set up a new file system. Can I start right now?"

Venus #1: "You can handle change much better than I can, so I wish you well—but I do envy you the money."

Venus #2: "As you know, I rarely have trouble getting along with people, so I have no problem. Do you think we can get a new paint job?"

Mars: "It really doesn't matter to me; I do my own thing anyway and intend to keep on doing it. Any objections?"

Jupiter: "I know you'll probably get bogged down the way you always do, so I'll help out by giving you some of my ideas. Want to hear some?"

Saturn: "I guess my time hasn't come yet, but I really don't envy you. You've got a tough row to hoe."

Uranus: "Oh, hadn't you heard? I'm transferring to new-product development. You'll miss me? Can't imagine why."

Neptune: "I've got mixed emotions, and I'd like to talk to you privately. How about a drink after work?"

Pluto: "I think it best I don't say anything."
Best bet for the sun: Mars.
Worst bet for the sun: Pluto.

2. Central Planet: The Moon

The moon recently ran an ad in the local newspaper which read: "Shy, lonely single looking for pleasing partner. Must be sensitive, intelligent, and thoughtful. Object: Marriage, home, and children." These are some of the answers she received:

Sun: "I don't usually answer ads, and I'm very popular. But I think it's time I settled down. Call me sometime."

Another moon: "I've been looking all my life for someone who understands me; if I don't hear from you in two days, I'll know you don't care."

Mercury #1: "I'll be sociable for the two of us; but I don't know about the children bit. They can tie you down."

Mercury #2: "You sound like the quiet type, which is fine with me, but I hope you like a clean house and nutritional food."

Venus #1: "I am a stable, home-loving person, and it sounds as if we would be good together—if sex is as important to you as it is to me."

Venus #2: "I can't tell from your ad what your tastes are; I know I can be a 'pleasing partner'—as long as the surroundings are right."

Mars: "I don't know if I would describe myself as sensitive, but I've got to meet you anyway. How soon can we make a date?"

Jupiter: "Nothing ventured, nothing gained. I'll take a chance on love with you, if you'll give me lots of space."

Saturn: "I have lots of money and it sounds as if you've got everything else I want. What does your father do?"

Uranus: "To be honest, the whole thing sounds dull. Do you have any friends?"

Neptune: "I think I know what you're looking for, and I can help you find it."

Pluto: "If you are really all you say, I'm desperately in love; just don't break your promise."
  Best bet for the moon: Venus #1.
  Worst bet for the moon: Mars.

3. Central Planet: Mercury #1

Light-hearted, sociable Mercury is giving a party, to which are invited a variety of friends and acquaintances. As Mercury circulates the room, Mercury asks: "What's the most interesting book you've read lately/movie you've seen/thing you've heard?"

Sun: "I haven't been reading much. I've been too busy writing my autobiography. Want to read the manuscript?"

Moon: "I'm fascinated by *Remembrance of Things Past*, but it makes me want to cry. Got a Kleenex?"

Another Mercury #1: "I've got so much to talk about we could go on all night. Any possibility of your getting out of here?"

Mercury #2: "I can tell you what's wrong with any current book or movie you can name. Want to name one? I should have been a critic, you know."

Venus #1: "I don't go out much, and what I really enjoy is listening to music and eating chocolate."

Venus #2: "This is a great party. Who does your catering?"

Mars: "Did you hear they gave the Most Valuable Player award to the wimp, Joey D.? It makes my blood boil."

Jupiter: "Have you heard the one about the priest and the procurer? It's a real knee-slapper."

Saturn: "I'm just catching up with Burton's *Anatomy of Melancholy*. It has so much to say about the current human situation, and the way I feel most of the time."

Uranus: "There's an experiment going on in the southeastern quadrant of New Zealand which will eventually prove that sheep have more need for each other than people do."

Neptune: "Where are the snows of yesteryear, where have they gone?"

Pluto: "I can't talk about it in this crowd."
    Best bet for Mercury #1: Venus #2.
    Worst bet for Mercury #1: The moon.

4. Central Planet: Mercury #2

This planet is a worrier, so Mercury #2 has decided to find out *exactly* what each of the neighbors thinks about the way he or she maintains his or her property:

Sun: "Except for the way you yell at the children, you're a model neighbor. Did you know I'm running for mayor?"

Moon: "Your place is spotless, but I don't think you're happy. Let's talk."

Mercury #1: "Glad you called, I'm putting together a little party ... Your property? Relax."

Another Mercury #2: "Why are you asking? Am I doing something wrong?"

Venus #1: "Wish I could keep a place so neat. Love your garden ... how are your tomatoes doing?"

Venus #2: "I haven't any complaints."

Mars: "You're a crab, and the whole neighborhood knows it."

Jupiter: "Live and let live, I always say. I'm going to add on to my place. What to hear my plans?"

Saturn: "It's very comforting to have a solid citizen like you for a neighbor. What do you hear about me?"

Uranus: "How did you know I was thinking of starting a neighborhood association?"

Neptune: "No man is an island. The fence? Can't say I've really noticed."

Pluto: "I feel it's something we should discuss on a one-to-one basis. When can we meet?"
   Best bet for Mercury #2: The moon.
   Worst bet for Mercury #2: Jupiter.

5. Central Planet: Venus #1

This attractive planet has no lack of admirers. Lately Venus #1 has had a series of blind dates, and has asked each to wind up the evening at his or her place. Here are the responses each gave to Venus #1's provocative invitation.

Sun: "Delighted. I could tell you wanted more of my company."

Moon: "Let me think about what kind of mood I'm in."

Mercury #1: "Sorry, I've got a late date. Next time?"

Mercury #2: "Only if you've got some aspirins. I've got a headache."

Another Venus #1: "Love to; I haven't had dessert."

Venus #2: "If I say no, will you get mad?"

Mars: "I thought you'd never ask."

Jupiter: "It's been nice, but I've got to run. I feel a touch of claustrophobia coming on."

Saturn: "It's late and I've got to get up early; but I feel so comfortable with you I'll come."

Uranus: "Why don't we go for a midnight bike ride instead?"

Neptune: "I have the feeling we could talk all night."

Pluto: "I've been feeling the magnetism all evening. I may never go home."

Best bet for Venus #1: Saturn.
Worst bet for Venus #1: Venus #2.

6. Central Planet: Venus #2

Genial, noncontroversial Venus #2 has reluctantly taken on the task of getting out the vote for a local candidate. In this case, it is Venus #2's *responses* that indicate the potential relationship with each of the answering planets.

Sun: "They should be supporting a person with leadership qualities, like me."
"Of course."

Moon: "My gut feelings tell me he doesn't have his heart in the right place."
"*Who* told you?"

Mercury #1: "I heard him speak the other night; I like his style."
"Yes, he does make a good appearance."

Mercury #2: "I've heard some things about him I don't like."
"Nobody's perfect."

Venus #1: "Nobody's going to tell *me* who to vote for."
"I'm only suggesting."

Another Venus #2: "What do you think?"
"I don't know—what do you think?"

Mars: "I want to see some action in this town. Is he a fighter?"
"I hope not; I hate violence."

Jupiter: "Frankly, he sounds like a jerk. What are you doing working for him?"
"Only my civic duty."

Saturn: "Where does he stand on taxes?"
"What an intelligent question!"

Uranus: "I'm organizing for the opposition candidate; your man is too conservative."
"Perhaps his suits are a bit dull."

Neptune: "I don't pay much attention to politics."
"Sorry to have bothered you."

Pluto: "I don't sense conviction in your voice."
"Do you want me to talk louder?"
Best bet for Venus #2: The sun.
Worst bet for Venus #2: Neptune.

7. Central Planet: Mars

Mars is dying to try hang-gliding and has decided to do it on the spur of the moment. In looking for a companion, Mars gets these responses from various friends.

Sun: "Piece of cake, but I can't make it today."

Moon: "You'll never get me up in one of those things ... but what a great sensation it must be."

Mercury #1: "Rather not do it myself, but can I come along and take pictures?"

Mercury #2: "Are you sure all that fresh air is really good for you?"

Venus #1: "Sounds exhausting; why don't you come over to dinner afterward?"

Venus #2: "What shall I wear?"

Another Mars: "Anything you can do I can do better. When do we leave?"

Jupiter: "Sensational idea. Maybe we can teach each other a few things."

Saturn: "I'd rather not, but what can you tell me about the investment possibilities connected with the sport?"

Uranus: "Sure I'll go, but it's old hat. Have you tried it with just one wing?"

Neptune: "I may be able to get it together by this afternoon. I'll call you back this time, I promise."

Pluto: "Let's have a contest."
  Best bet for Mars: Jupiter.
  Worst bet for Mars: Saturn.

8. Central Planet: Jupiter

Jupiter has just come back from an extended trip abroad and is trying to put together a group of people to see his or her slides; Jupiter's offering a potluck supper and a prize to the person who can correctly identify all of the subjects. Here's what Jupiter gets back from the people invited:

Sun: "The last time you were the only one who got to say anything."

Moon: "I hope this doesn't hurt your feelings, but slide shows make me nervous."

Mercury #1: "Can I bring some of my slides, too? There's plenty I haven't shown you."

Mercury #2: "Give me a little time to think about it."

Venus #1: "I was planning to spend a quiet evening at home, but I'll come if we can spend a little time by ourselves later."

Venus #2: "Who else will be there?"

Mars: "Hell, no. I'd rather see things in person."

Another Jupiter: "Are you going to drone on like the last time? I'll bring a bottle."

Saturn: "How much is the prize?"

Uranus: "I've just discovered a great new lens. Can I see if it works on your projector?"

Neptune: "I would love to experience the beauty you have seen. I'll try not to be late."

Pluto: "I think you've got something up your sleeve. What's the catch?"
  Best bet for Jupiter: Mercury #1.
  Worst bet for Jupiter: Pluto.

9. Central Planet: Saturn

Saturn has been hospitalized with a bad case of exhaustion from overwork. While patient with his present condition, he is terribly concerned about how things are going back at the office, where he is president and chief financial officer. He asks each of his visitors from the office the same question: "Should I be worried about anything?"

Sun: "Relax; I've taken over and everything is going splendidly. In fact, morale seems even better than before."

Moon: "Now don't you worry about a thing; you'll just make yourself sicker, and I couldn't stand how that would make me feel."

Mercury #1: "We're all having a ball. Want to hear the latest gossip?"

Mercury #2: "I'm worrying for the two of us. What was our first symptom? You see, I've got this funny pain . . ."

Venus #1: "I can't imagine why, but people keep coming to me with their troubles. You wouldn't believe the work!"

Venus #2: "You look wonderful! By the way, I certainly hope your little problem won't delay our bonuses."

Mars: "What a relief not having you around, you drag! Ha, ha . . . only kidding."

Jupiter: "Now I'm taking the liberty of putting that little plan of mine in action. What's the matter? . . . Nurse! Nurse!"

Another Saturn: "Can't bear to think what first-quarter profits will look like. Is this a well-run hospital?"

Uranus: "Let's approach this thing logically. First, let's look at the accounts we don't have to worry about, then . . ."

Neptune: "Let's step back and look at the larger picture. In today's socioeconomic climate . . ."

Pluto: "Don't listen to what anyone else tells you. I'm the one who has the situation under control."

Best bet for Saturn: Uranus.
Worst bet for Saturn: Mercury #1.

10. Central Planet: Uranus

This rather impersonal planet sometimes plunges in where others fear to tread. He is conducting a telephone survey on the sex habits of the community in which he lives; he will later publish it through the university where he teaches sociology. In attempting to prove that virtually no one is wedded to traditional attitudes these days, he asks two questions: "Do you consider yourself a good sex partner?" and "What is the most innovative thing you do in bed?"

Sun: "I am pretty good, if I have to say so myself. Are you going to use my name?"

Moon: "It's much too emotional a subject for me to discuss over the phone; doesn't it make *you* uncomfortable?"

Mercury #1: "What a good idea—wish I'd thought of it. Can I write up your results for the local paper?"

Mercury #2: "I pride myself on doing everything perfectly. As for the second question, didn't you ever hear that Virgo is the most experimental sign in the zodiac?"

Venus #1: "I never thought about it much. I just do it and love it . . . *everything*."

Venus #2: "I really don't know what you're talking about."

Mars: "Did you ever hear of a sexual athlete? Let me tell you how I . . ."

Jupiter: "Anything goes among friends."

Saturn: "I try to keep up with all the latest techniques, but there's so much to read I get confused when I try to do it."

Another Uranus: "Just a minute, I'll go get my notes."

Neptune: "Did you ever try doing it to Debussy's 'La Mer'? What a high!"

Pluto: "If I told you you wouldn't believe it—so I'll keep it to myself."
Best bet for Uranus: Mercury #2.
Worst bet for Uranus: The moon.

11. Central Planet: Neptune

This mystical planet loves to get out of this world, and will take every opportunity to. Neptune has discovered a new medium and wants to have a seance. Here's how Neptune's friends react:

Sun: "Sorry; I've got a PTA meeting. Call me next time you want to play cards."

Moon: "I've heard wonderful things about her; I'll bring the candles and incense."

Mercury #1: "Whom are we going to try to contact?"

90

Mercury #2: "You know, it's not healthy for all those people to sit around in an airless room holding hands."

Venus #1: "You really believe in that stuff, huh?"

Venus #2: "Seances are terribly romantic; I'll come."

Mars: "You're kidding."

Jupiter: "How fascinating! I share your interest in the metaphysical, but I hope it doesn't take too long."

Saturn: "Life is difficult enough in this world. Think I'll pass it up."

Uranus: "Good. This will give me an opportunity to test the theory of electrobiomagnetic intergalactic energy."

Another Neptune: "There are more things in this world than most people dream of. I'll bring some hash."

Pluto: "I'll join the circle, but I can't be responsible for anything that happens."
  Best bet for Neptune: Venus #2.
  Worst bet for Neptune: The sun.

12. Central Planet: Pluto

This passionate planet has had a serious affair with a number of people in the office, but is never satisfied. Here's how the rest react to Pluto's subtle but seductive approach, which begins, "Do you sense the magnetism between us?"

Sun: "It's good to know you find me attractive, but I'm attached."

Moon: "I'm sure a lot of people don't understand you, but I do."

Mercury #1: "I just thought it was warm in here."

Mercury #2: "You have an annoying habit of putting your hands on people. Please don't touch me."

Venus #1: "Is that what it is? I call it something else. See you after work."

Venus #2: "What a lovely voice you have. Please pass the sugar."

Mars: "Buzz off before I show you how my magnetism works."

Jupiter: "I don't think we have a thing in common, but let's give it a whirl anyway."

Saturn: "But what about my family ... my job ... my future?"

Uranus: "Sorry, I don't get involved, but what do you call that theory?"

Neptune: "Yes, it's absolutely spiritual, but I don't want to get hurt."

Another Pluto: "We'd end up destroying each other; anyway, I've got something else going. Well, OK."
Best bet for Pluto: Pluto.
Worst bet for Pluto: Mercury #2.

SCORPIO DAY-BY-DAY
PREDICTIONS, 1984

January 1984

Astronote to Scorpio: It would be almost impossible to overemphasize the critical importance of this year to the sign of Scorpio. The planetary lineup is such that it virtually guarantees a year of significant developments. Pluto—the outermost planet and ruler of Scorpio—has just moved into its own sign after a long-term stay in the sign of Libra. What this means for Scorpio is a long-term trend—a period of years in which members of this sign (self-involved under any planetary conditions) will find a deepening involvement and interest in self-transformation. Along with Pluto, the "tester" planet Saturn makes a pass through Scorpio, returning to that sign after about twenty-nine years. In plain terms the message to Scorpio is this: take it slow and steady and don't get rattled. The challenges that come your way this year will be real ones, but each one has "opportunity" written on its flip side. If you find yourself getting carried away with a lust for power or any other potentially destructive emotion, take a deep breath and think again. You always know how to go after what you want and very often you get it. It isn't necessary to turn up your emotional temperature any higher. Use your considerable powers of self-control to keep things in perspective. You will have a lot of help from the normally effusive planet Jupiter whose tendency to excess is tempered by the sign of Capricorn which Jupiter inhabits this year. In short, 1984 can be the best of years or the worst of years for powerful Scorpio. As always, the choice is yours whether to play the heavy or act the saint.

Sunday, January 1: Some of your New Year's resolutions concern your financial status. Get out the sharp pencil and start figuring where to draw the line in order to increase assets and decrease deficits. You will be negotiating with others and should listen to their suggestions as well.

Monday, January 2: You are not always delighted to have drop-in guests, but this one is especially welcome for making a great suggestion about redecorating your digs. It may involve a luxury purchase, but will do so much for your surroundings it is worth it. The lucky number is 6.

Tuesday, January 3: There are a lot of cross currents today and it may take a bit of doing to keep everything straight in your mind. It would help to get *everyone* to agree on terms; semantics are often at the root of confusion. Also, get all the material in order first so that you will have everything on hand.

Wednesday, January 4: Someone may be trying to pressure you into doing things his or her way; the way you look at it, someone is trying to pull your strings and it irritates you. Don't get mad; get even. Just smile sweetly and say "thanks" for the advice, but follow your own instincts. Whose responsibility is it anyway?

Thursday, January 5: Don't miss a trick today because what you are involved in may be critical to your security. Because part of it is tedious, you may be tempted to "skim"; it is important to be as precise as possible. You will be glad when it's over. Then you will have time to broaden your horizons.

Friday, January 6: Out with the old, in with the new! You can't stick with the same old way of doing things now; a fresh approach is sorely needed—as if anyone had to tell you. It may be rough going now, but in the long run you will be delighted when you begin to feel brand new.

Saturday, January 7: It's your turn to give your all for someone who helped you out when you needed it; you haven't forgotten how grateful you were. There may be a family discussion about a whole new regime in diet, cooking and meals. Try to reach agreement and start out on the right foot. The luck number is 2.

Sunday, January 8: You should be lighthearted today and feel like having some fun. Be sure to include some children or young people. Some good news may lift your spirits even higher and you will have plenty to talk about with some chatty friends who normally find you a bit quiet.

Monday, January 9: It's hard to keep your cool today and you may feel like somebody or something has you trapped. Deal with your impatience and realize that there's a testing process going on. You may not like the tactics but you have to go along. Don't scowl when you are asked to redo something you thought was over and done with.

Tuesday, January 10: Fortunately you get some kind of outlet today and you can work off that excess psychic energy. You are among much more compatible people and get genuinely interested in some health and diet practices you hear about. The lucky number is 5.

Wednesday, January 11: Take a low-key approach today in a delicate matter; if you force the issue you will get nothing but backlash. One way to be conciliatory is to keep a promise you made a while back. Everything cools down by evening and harmony is restored.

Thursday, January 12: Hold back when you are tempted to speak out and commit yourself; you don't need to feel rushed because time is on your side. Appear to bend a little and by the time the matter must be decided the weight of opinion will be on your side. The answer will not come today.

97

Friday, January 13: A really big opportunity comes along today and let's hope you recognize it for what it is. A lot more responsibility may be involved, but the potential rewards for shrewd Scorpio are enormous. Others with your kind of style are involved.

Saturday, January 14: Get rid of something that's holding you back; you don't need the situation or the person anymore, and you are carrying an unnecessary burden. It's time for some creative selfishness—which is not as bad as it sounds. In the long run you will be happier and the ones you really care about will benefit.

Sunday, January 15: Your energy returns with a bang and some news you get lifts your spirits. You can afford to be optimistic now if you are very careful to scrutinize every area where you can turn a profit. The lucky number today is 1.

Mid-month memo to Scorpio: If you are in the doldrums about this time of the year, you can rekindle your spark by dabbling in a typically Scorpio hobby or activity. Here are some you might try:

Buy a few new detective novels; take a course in first aid; study magic and learn some tricks; check out your insurance policies; clean the cellar; join the volunteer ambulance corps; get a book on archeology and plan to go on a dig; go into group therapy; start an insect collection; get active in local politics; work at the poison control center; buy, read, or see something X-rated; do your taxes; join a reform movement; hold a séance; read up on the occult; study your family's genealogy; go on an ocean voyage.

Monday, January 16: Though it's a rather small one, you are glad when your ship comes in today. It inspires you to take inventory of everything you have, and to get some professional advice if you are in doubt about the value of things.

98

Tuesday, January 17: Your mind is on higher things today, and you are able to lift your eyes from what is close at hand. You may start devising a plan that involves travel and feel yourself getting excited about it already. You also might decide to study a foreign language. The lucky number is 3.

Wednesday, January 18: The train of thought that started rolling yesterday gets a full head of steam today. You are so eager to talk about your ideas that you get in touch with people at a distance. They too share your enthusiasm and could make great partners for your anticipated venture.

Thursday, January 19: You get a leg up on the competition today when your prestige becomes greater. It changes your standing for the better among your immediate group and it is an honor others envy. Don't let them make you feel any less great than you should feel.

Friday, January 20: Someone whose "brains" you admire gives you a pat on the back and it is very gratifying. On another front, you must conform to the will of others. It is an adjustment for you, but you realize it is the only sensible course. The lucky number is 6.

Saturday, January 21: Even a Scorpio can be naïve at times, and this time you really are not getting what is really going on. It's important to look at things as they are—not as you wish them to be. You can do this and still keep an open mind. Meanwhile, a friendship could develop into something far stronger—and sexier.

Sunday, January 22: It's great to have friends—and even better when they can do something for you. The fulfillment of a dream for you can be made possible through the help of another—and it looks as if it will happen. You feel particularly hopeful and much more secure.

Monday, January 23: Your good deeds in the past keep coming back to you; today it's in the form of very valuable assistance from an old pal you helped once. It is a pleasant day in which you feel rather outgoing and delighted to interact with the people around you. The lucky number is 9.

Tuesday, January 24: The clouds that have been obscuring a situation suddenly lift and you are able to see what has really been happening. It's a relief to at least be informed. Spend some quiet time mulling things over and you will be able to put it into perspective. Pick up the phone and call someone who would get a lift from hearing from you.

Wednesday, January 25: MOON IN SCORPIO. Each month the moon passes through all twelve signs in the zodiac; today it enters yours. What that means for you is a feeling of buoyancy and the ability to express yourself clearly and with impact. You get a hunch today and you should follow through with it because your judgment is running high.

Thursday, January 26: The moon in your sign aids you in showing others just how flexible and versatile you can be. Your reputation for sometimes being a bit on the down side does not hold today as you display your delightful if sardonic sense of humor. The lucky number is 3.

Friday, January 27: Money talks today and helps you get your points across. You are in a strong position and should resolve to keep yourself there by paying close attention to the little things that mean so much in transactions like this. Check the fine print.

Saturday, January 28: Several nice things happen to you today. One is a tip you receive that could put you ahead in the money game. The other is a compliment on how good you look from a member of the opposite sex. It should make you aware that appearances do count and deserve more attention than you are sometimes willing to give.

Sunday, January 29: Don't go it alone today; a close family member should be included in an important discussion that really involves him or her. This gesture of consideration and conciliation will help resolve a tense situation that has arisen. Surround yourself with clear thinkers for best results.

Monday, January 30: If you gloss over some suspicions you have about a certain individual, you will be fooling yourself. It is important to be realistic even if it means something you want badly may be delayed; you will get far better results if you get more information before you proceed.

Tuesday, January 31: Face it: someone you have been fairly close to is trying to get more involved with you. Consider whether or not you want the relationship to intensify any further. Listen to some good old-fashioned advice someone with more experience can give you; there's nothing like having been there.

February 1984

Astronote to Scorpio: Scorpio may not outwardly appear to take Valentine's Day very seriously—but chances are that beneath your outer "cool" there is a lot of passion and even cool Scorpio loves Valentine's Day.

Tangible displays of affection are extremely important to this sensitive sign. "Sensitive?" you may ask. "I thought Scorpio was as tough as nails." Sensitivity doesn't necessarily mean softness; what Scorpio's brand of sensitivity resembles is a ticking time bomb. When the desperately wanted and desperately needed gestures of love are received, the countdown will end before zero hour. However, if Scorpio is slighted—and you are the slighter—stand back for a pretty big explosion. Not that Scorpio would literally hurt you; in fact, the violence of Scorpio's emotions are usually most hurtful to him or herself. The one who gets involved with a member of this sign quickly learns that you never kid a Scorpio about love because in matters of the heart, he or she has virtually no sense of humor. "Serious" is the word that best describes most of Scorpio's love entanglements, so you might as well be prepared to play it straight. On the other hand, among the many wonderful things the Scorpio's loved one gets in return is the kind of love most of us would feel lucky to get. It is deep, passionate, and sincere—and that's *far* from being bad. Just remember that while Scorpio loves *deeply*, he or she does not love *eternally*.

Wednesday, February 1: Your thoughts are on rather basic security matters today; you and someone you live with are trying to establish a new order with which you both feel comfortable. There is an adjustment involved, but your attitude is quite positive because some unexpected funds become available.

Thursday, February 2: You really believe someone is sincere; but you must realize that he or she has not been totally filled in. Therefore, be gentle but firm, when you have to say "thanks, but no thanks." Let the person know you have to be cautious in this matter The lucky number is 7.

Friday, February 3: If you have ever thought about going into business for yourself, today is a day to consider it carefully. It's your own powerful personality that gives you an edge, and the possibility of very solid backing. If you are not ready for that now, put it in your mental file for a later date.

Saturday, February 4: Again today you find that you have people coming to you with offers of support—both emotional and financial. It should give your ego a boost to know you have such appeal. Don't neglect to finish up something that needs doing, however. It's fun to be lionized but don't let it go to your head.

Sunday, February 5: Those Scorpio sensors are really working today and they pick up some very good vibes from a member of the opposite sex. It could mean the beginning of something big for you. Remember, however, your vow to increase your independence and then decide whether or not this fits in. The lucky number is 1.

Monday, February 6: You usually learn from experience, so remind yourself of some recent lessons today. It will serve you well in dealing with a rather intricate problem that involves financial or emotional security. Take the safe route no matter how tempted you are to dash off in a new direction.

Tuesday, February 7: It's good for you to socialize with new groups of people, so accept an invitation that comes your way today. You can control your urge to overdo in food and drink and still have a great time. You will get some brand-new insights and ideas.

Wednesday, February 8: Sometimes you feel as if the whole world depends on you and today is one of those days. Demands and requests come from all sides. Do what you can but be a little firm with people you think should take more on their shoulders.

Thursday, February 9: You are freed up today and able to get a little variety into your life—which may be badly needed at this point. Investigate some interesting opportunities to make changes, but be very aware of the rights of others—particularly marital partners.

Friday, February 10: It's not up to you to make the first move, so contain yourself. If you act hastily you will blow the whole deal. Let the other side put its cards on the table first. It may even be wise to give in on a couple of points now in order to put yourself in a better position later on.

Saturday, February 11: Don't let anyone fast-talk you today—including yourself. A realistic point of view is essential if not particularly inspiring. You really can do more with what you have by being very clever about making special deals, etc. Stick to the facts, but try your luck with number 7.

Sunday, February 12: All kinds of obligations may weigh heavily on your mind today, but console yourself with the knowledge that you have a lot of people on your side. Don't be hesitant to accept their help. You have gotten too close to things and could use a few objective pairs of eyes.

Monday, February 13: You start off the week in much better spirits and some of those around you are relieved. An optimistic attitude makes you realize you can get much further if you make the right moves. It's a good idea to take every opportunity to communicate with people who have know-how. Don't be shy.

Tuesday, February 14: This should be one of the nicest Valentine's Days you have had in years, because true romance is indicated. So is a really fun party that marks the occasion. Get in there and mingle and try your luck with number 1.

Wednesday, February 15: It's great to have your goals in sight again and to know exactly where you are going. Your intuition is running high, so you are able to smell out an opportunity and grab it. You also grab more responsibility at the same time.

Mid-month memo to Scorpio: It must be a bit disconcerting to Scorpio that every time the sign is mentioned people raise an eyebrow and look knowing. The silent message is "sexy but scary." True, the sign is complicated with regard to matters of the heart, but good, solid relationships are not impossible with Scorpio types. Some say it takes a Scorpio to handle a Scorpio, and there may be some truth in the statement; however, the involvement could be mutually destructive as well. The more malleable sign of Cancer is a better bet. As a water sign, Cancer understands the complexity of those driven by emotions, but will generally be the one to bend. Pisces with Scorpio is a potential disaster, however.

The earth signs hold more possibilities for Scorpio, and Capricorn is an excellent partner. Both signs are driven to succeed and prosper materially, though their motives are different. They will find mutual satisfaction in what they build and amass. Taurus too could be happy in Scorpio's "nest," but might get trampled from time to time.

The fire signs offer one good candidate for love-hungry Scorpio, and that is Aries. The Aries lover will take no nonsense and will refuse to be pushed around; in fact, he or she will push right back. Though the relationship will be stormy, it will provide a comfortable battleground for both parties. Leo is too self-involved to be happy with self-involved Scorpio and Sagittarius will not even comprehend what all the Scorpio fuss is about.

The air sign that has the best shot at a happy relationship with Scorpio is Aquarius. A fixed sign like Scorpio, and therefore as determined, Aquarius is also able to look objectively at Scorpio's passionate likes and dislikes and even clarify them to Scorpio's benefit. The air sign Gemini is much too light for Scorpio and Libra would find Scorpio's emotionalism much too messy for comfort.

Thursday, February 16: There is cause for celebration and it may temporarily take you away from more serious things. You need the diversion and will find lots of stimulation from the people you celebrate with. An absolute inspiration comes into your head!

Friday, February 17: Today you take on a challenge that's a little scary, but you do it well and in the process make a new friend. You feel exhilarated; isn't it great to be popular? Romance is a distinct possibility as well.

Saturday, February 18: You have keen analytical powers, so put them to good use today. Don't let someone bamboozle you with glib and superficial explanations; find out what his or her real motive is. You get a nice gesture of love and affection from a member of the opposite sex.

Sunday, February 19: Retire into your own little private world today for a period of rest and reflection. The world has been a bit too much with you of late. In your temporary confinement you will be able to get back your perspective and some badly needed psychic energy.

Monday, February 20: Someone asks you to join an inner circle today and you find you gain access to some confidential information. It is inspiring in a way you are not used to, but that is good for you. Visit a confined friend in the hospital or at home. The lucky number is 7.

Tuesday, February 21: MOON IN SCORPIO. Today you come out of your shell and blink because the world seems so bright. Money is one issue that takes a turn for the better and you are amazed that you are rewarded for your recent hard work. It really does pay off!

Wednesday, February 22: You are able to dump something that's been a bother recently and move forward in a less inhibited way. It's great to get the green light for something you have been dying to do. Some people who think the way you do are terrific companions at this time.

Thursday, February 23: Today you jump feet first into your new project and ask questions that test the waters. Your need to make new contacts may take you on a short side trip. You are eager and ready to do so because your enthusiasm is so great. The lucky number is 1.

Friday, February 24: You get a flash today that gives you the right answer as if out of nowhere; it's really your intuition working in high gear. You are in a good spot to increase the thickness of your wallet if you play your cards right. Some pretty shrewd people could be competitors.

Saturday, February 25: You will be running around in circles today, but they will be interesting ones. A lot of information is coming your way from a lot of different sources. One is a new contact you make that seems casual—but may not be in the long run. The lucky number is 3.

Sunday, February 26: You are building bridges now and it is wise to do so—particularly with relatives. It is always a secure feeling to know there are people there for you when you need them. Someone may pay you a surprise visit, but in this case you are delighted rather than flustered.

Monday, February 27: You get some pretty gratifying playback on something you submitted recently. You know that at least you are in the running. A surge of good feelings puts you in a playful mood, and you find there are those who are delighted to join you in some recreation.

Tuesday, February 28: The mood you are in is quite serious contrasted to yesterday's; in fact, you may be downright angry. You know you can protect your rights in a certain situation, but it is aggravating to have to get involved. Someone in your circle needs your help, however, so involvement is unavoidable.

Wednesday, February 29: Once again you are aware that someone is trying to put something over on you, and you are not about to play the fool. Just define your terms very clearly. Some people are not always as scrupulous as you are in money matters.

March 1984

Astronote to Scorpio: Scorpio is probably the most misunderstood sign in the zodiac. Usually dismissed as too complicated (or downright dangerous), the sign does not often enjoy the benefit of the doubt from others. To really comprehend what makes Scorpio tick, it is useful to look at the sign's position in the zodiac. The eighth sign of twelve, Scorpio belongs to the second half of the "magic circle" and is therefore destined to have to deal with others as much as with self. The "emerging soul" that the whole zodiac represents is in Scorpio at a very difficult stage—still pulling away from childhood and yet still not totally grown up.

In terms of the individual, this symbolism translates into the typical Scorpio's often petulant behavior. Part of Scorpio is pulled inward toward self and self-gratification; the other part is pulled outward toward the concerns of others. What typically happens is that the Scorpio person tries at once to control him or herself *and* outside circumstances—a pretty tricky assignment. That uncomfortable feeling people sometimes get in the presence of Scorpio comes from the fact that Scorpio is usually trying to extend his or her sphere of influence and draw others into it too. Scorpio finds it hard to leave well enough alone and has not yet learned how to say this too shall pass. It is difficult for Scorpio to figure out when the battle is over—or to even *consider* the fact that he or she may not have won. Yes, Scorpio is egotistical—but it stems from a deep-seated conviction that he or she really can control the world—both his or her own and yours.

Thursday, March 1: Pretty basic matters of home and security occupy your time and your mind today, but you feel both interested and stimulated. You are able to see how the things you build today will develop in the future—and it is more than satisfying. For lighter activity, try your luck with number 7.

Friday, March 2: It's one of those days when you should look over your shoulder; someone is rather envious of you and could try to cause trouble. You are way out in front, however, so know that he or she isn't a threat. At the same time, keep your eye on the brass ring in front of you; it will be within reach soon.

Saturday, March 3: Your senses are keen and your mind sharp today; you have a "vision." Be firm in your resolve to get what you want—even if it means extra effort and a possible trip. You can be unusually determined when you want to, and this is one of those times it will pay off.

Sunday, March 4: Right on! Today you are able to toss out some old ideas and thinking habits to make room for your independent new stance. You may literally clean out closets or home files as well. You feel revved up and ready to meet new people; get a new start. The lucky number is 1.

Monday, March 5: Today you get a signal to slow down and it comes in the form of a family matter that needs attention. No matter how eager you are to get on with it in terms of your own needs, you must defer to the needs of others now. You should still keep thinking about your master plan in the meantime, however. In fact, you get a great hunch that will serve you well.

Tuesday, March 6: You feel exceptionally well and fit today. It puts you in such a good frame of mind that you are able to display your wonderfully witty sense of humor. It puts some people on notice that you have a lot more to you than is immediately apparent. Remember to dip into your reserves of versatility more often.

Wednesday, March 7: You get a wonderful opportunity to renegotiate something today; plan your moves very carefully. If necessary, rehearse your presentation of your wants or needs. You don't have to play the heavy, however. You may be amazed to find how easy some people are to deal with.

Thursday, March 8: Your mate or partner surprises you today with a rather direct question and/or demand. It means a change, but you are intrigued with the idea. Give it a lot of due consideration, but remember that in the long run it's you who has to decide. After all, whose life is it anyway?

Friday, March 9: Someone around you has been doing a time-and-motion study and offers a plan for greater efficiency. It makes a lot of sense. Show your gratitude for the extra effort he or she put in. The lucky number is 6 today.

Saturday, March 10: If you feel that you never get a break, today you are proved wrong. In fact, you get a rare opportunity to get in on something you thought had passed by long ago. Grab it! You will be in on a deal with some pretty solid citizens, and you will enjoy the company.

Sunday, March 11: Today you dream very possible dreams, which could include travel, study—or both. You find yourself getting very excited about the prospects and enjoy brainstorming with some others who have a similar plan. One person has a great idea for funding the endeavor.

Monday, March 12: Easy does it is the keynote of the day. You find obstacles seem to fade away and people around you are unusually supportive. It should occur to you that your positive frame of mind has a lot to do with the pleasant atmosphere. Resolve to remember this lesson when you get really down.

Tuesday, March 13: Cooperative efforts are paying off now and you put together a super team today. Together you are able to get a new thing going and to outline your objectives clearly. You are the one with the golden touch today in terms of communication, so offer to be the one to put it in writing.

Wednesday, March 14: A very substantial "pat on the back" comes your way from someone higher up. He or she actually asks what *you* would do in the situation. Respond with interest and vigor; the impression you make is like money in the bank for the future. Feel confident and look the part.

Thursday, March 15: You should feel flattered by an invitation that comes your way today; it indicates your prestige among people who count in your scheme of things. It's a fabulous chance not only to meet new people, but also to exchange ideas and score points by displaying your ability and versatility.

Mid-month memo to Scorpio: Over thousands of years astrologers have refined and sifted the knowledge they have gained about each sign and come up with some general principles that govern the behavior of each.

111

Complicated Scorpio looks a little easier to understand when you see the key factors in the Scorpio "equation." They are:

Compulsion; exploration; preservation; control; force; courage; renewing; elimination; purification; subterranean things; crisis; solitude; growth; patience; procreation; endurance; the will; patience; dynamism; aloneness; anonymity; purging; intensity; death; rebirth; self-control; aggressiveness; fearlessness.

Friday, March 16: Your mind is on very personal matters today, specifically a person of the opposite sex. Much to your delight and surprise, that individual lets you know—in no uncertain terms—that you are appreciated. It gives you a big lift and makes a tough job you have to do a lot easier.

Saturday, March 17: It's like a wish come true! You are getting much closer to someone you have been admiring from afar. There is a significant change in the tenor of the relationship and it suits you just fine. In another matter, don't forget some important paperwork that needs doing. The lucky number is 5.

Sunday, March 18: Lay back and put your Scorpio powers of X-ray vision to work today; you have to look beyond the obvious to get the answers you want. At the same time, don't neglect to give some much-needed TLC to a friend or family member who is a bit down in the dumps—possibly because of illness.

Monday, March 19: You are in a mood to be tough with yourself—if not others. Some resolutions you made not too long ago to keep yourself in tip-top shape have gotten a little shaky. Willpower! In this frame of mind you are able to cast off some rosy thoughts you had about someone or something. You are right to be realistic.

Tuesday, March 20: MOON IN SCORPIO. This is an especially decisive day, both in terms of your ability to come to terms with things and in actual events. Your judgment and timing are excellent and a very significant boost to your career is indicated. In love, too, you can be forthright—and win the day.

Wednesday, March 21: You are able to take the direct approach again today and charm others into doing things your way. Your personality more than shines—it dazzles—and you should dress the part as well. Get out to see and be seen; it's time to come out of your shell.

Thursday, March 22: Some great news starts the day off with a bang! And it looks as if money is the subject. Whatever it is, you are in a mood to celebrate and will be looking for people to party with. Someone who generally turns you off wants to join you; it's more than okay when you find out just how delightful he or she can be.

Friday, March 23: You have your own way of doing things and are usually not pleased when someone tries to give you advice. Today you may have to listen to some from a family member. Don't close your mind; the benefit of experience can benefit you. The lucky number is 11.

Saturday, March 24: Trust only your own judgment today; it's not such a good idea to rely on others. You will have to do the driving—perhaps literally to see some relatives who have made a conciliatory gesture. A personal appearance is most important in putting the situation back to rights.

Sunday, March 25: The focus remains on family matters again today. This time it's your own place that may need some attention. Don't gloss over some important things that need doing; security should be uppermost in your mind. Don't let a breezy friend divert you from the tasks at hand.

Monday, March 26: Recent changes have freed you up, and it's nice to be able to move around a little—even if it only means freedom of thought. You are becoming aware of how important a purely intellectual relationship can be to you; it doesn't always have to be physical.

Tuesday, March 27: You get a real sense of satisfaction today when something is over and done with. It's nice to feel like a fat cat once in a while; at least for now you are secure. Some other people in the picture are compatible with your way of thinking.

Wednesday, March 28: Finally the boundary lines are drawn and you find that you are in a pretty good spot. The benefit of the doubt is in your direction. In the process you make some stimulating new contacts who could prove very useful in the future. The lucky number is 7.

Thursday, March 29: If you play your cards right you could successfully complete a major power play today. In this particular cycle it is easy for you to show your style in a most impressive manner. Whether it's money or love, you could be the victor today. Don't blow it!

Friday, March 30: It's possible that you are madly in love; don't get too carried away. This is a very sentimental day and you could be mistaking some romantic feelings for the real thing. On the other hand, the time is ripe for an adventure. Take it in that spirit!

Saturday, March 31: You are able to make great inroads today and get right to the bottom of things. There could be a showdown—a rather emotional one. Be sure to protect yourself, but don't be too harsh on others either. You *can* get rough. The lucky number is 1.

April 1984

Astronote to Scorpio: You have met the Scorpio lover in general; now what about the female of the species? The Scorpio woman as partner, wife, and mother is a fascinating study in contrasts; you might even say a paradox. The most sexual and sensual of women, in many cases she would prefer to have been born a man. Physically, she may be all woman, but if you think of her as all girl you are in for a rude shock. The Scorpio female is tough, in the best and the worst senses of the word. She has utter contempt for her "silly" sisters who think they need a man to lean on, and from her earliest years she has looked down her nose at the pink-and-white image that used to be standard for women. As a matter of fact, it was most likely Scorpio women who were the first at the barricades in the early days of women's liberation. The paradox is that the female Scorpio exudes come-hither sexuality; it's only when you get inside her head that you discover she's not quite as easy as you thought.

Even if she never leaves hearth and home for career and job success, the Scorpio woman is often the stronger partner in a relationship. It is her misfortune that since she refuses to be a leaner, she often attracts them as partners. When this happens, don't expect her to stay around long. The minute she realizes her mistake, she will exit stage left and vanish without a trace. On the other hand, in the right partnership no one is more loyal and passionately attached than the Scorpio female. When she meets her match, she is so fulfilled that she would not give him up for the world. Jealous? She may have invented the word. It is wise for the mate of a Scorpio woman to tread the straight and narrow; it was of her that was written "hell hath no fury like a woman scorned." She will hold up her end of the marital bargain superbly, and if by chance she finds a competing interest she will let you know about it and even give you a chance to come up to the mark.

If the Scorpio woman sounds a little tough to deal with, it is not surprising. Her black moods and violent temper are legendary. However, she has also been a bit maligned. Her passion is more than purely sexual and when she applies it to her role as wife and mother she has no peer in the zodiac. For one thing, she will treat her children with benign neglect. It is not indifference to their needs but a determination to raise them to be as independent and self-reliant as she. The Scorpio mother is a pusher, too; she will insist that her children develop the best that is in them. No slackers are allowed in her household. All things considered, the Scorpio female is a wonderful woman, and the man who wins her has taken a prize.

Sunday, April 1: The only one who is generally able to fool you is yourself; you may be fooling yourself now. Be absolutely realistic about what you see in an individual or a situation. Wishful thinking is not very productive—especially for you. Watch your diet too! The lucky number is 8.

Monday, April 2: You become the possessor of privileged information today; respect its confidentiality. It can be very useful to you, but it could be disastrous to someone else. Play fair. One thing it does is cement a relationship with someone who is now a good buddy.

Tuesday, April 3: As if sent from heaven, someone with lots of get-up-and-go comes along and takes a big weight off your shoulders. In another area try to be patient. If you take it slow and keep a low profile, the opportunity to act will be there soon.

Wednesday, April 4: To you it's elementary. Your ESP is running so high today you can see exactly what's going

116

on and what you have to do. Don't forget your public relations personality however; someone's nose could get out of joint. You don't really care, but it could be inconvenient because you need him or her on your side.

Thursday, April 5: You feel like asking a million questions today and you are uncharacteristically nosey. However, someone may actually ask you to stick your nose in his or her business. It's nice to have someone think you are smart enough to help. It gives you a new insight into money matters, too.

Friday, April 6: It's no mystery to you why someone has been acting a certain way; you took the trouble to find out. It helps you to be clear in your own mind while others are still floundering. You can get closer to him or her and it puts you closer to pay dirt. One stubborn person could cause you some headaches, however.

Saturday, April 7: Protect yourself—and your ideas. Sometimes you can be a little gullible and let others reap the benefit of your thinking. It is important to stay alert to the motives of some people who are not necessarily as friendly as they appear. The lucky number is 5.

Sunday, April 8: There is a bit of excitement on the home and family scene today as someone tells you about some plans that have been brewing. They involve you indirectly, but you would be interested anyway because you care about the person. Travel could be on your mind now.

Monday, April 9: A seed that was planted yesterday takes root today and you are inspired to move a travel plan forward. You may go so far as to make an itinerary, even though your plan is a rather long-range one. As you plan, keep your values in mind. Don't give up anything you really value for short-term gains.

Tuesday, April 10: The pressure is on, but you are ready for it. You quickly get your act together when a chance to move ahead is presented. You are right to grab the reins of a project because you have good backing and important people who support your position. Nice going!

Wednesday, April 11: You score high again today, and it's a good feeling to see that people are giving you the recognition you think you deserve. Don't get carried away with self-importance, however. You didn't really do it all alone. The lucky number is 9.

Thursday, April 12: You know it's time for a heart-to-heart and so does your opposite number. You both need to talk about giving each other more room; there is a spirit of independence on both sides. It's very possible to start off on a whole new footing and make things work. Don't overdo today.

Friday, April 13: Instead of the proverbial bad luck this day brings, you get a pleasant surprise. A group of your friends want to celebrate with you your recent stroke of luck. One person in particular delights you when he or she gives you a token of love and affection.

Saturday, April 14: You feel refreshed and renewed today; company is good for you. You find out that someone's been working behind the scenes in your behalf. Show your gratitude. You may feel inspired enough to turn a routine date into a romantic interlude.

Sunday, April 15: You find yourself among a circle of compatible people and you love the exchange of ideas because it gives you a few great ones. Part of the time you may have to seclude yourself to do some important paperwork; it's important not to neglect it. The lucky number is 4.

Mid-month memo to Scorpio: The worst sin you can commit against a Scorpio woman is to ignore her need to be taken seriously. The best way to win her over is to engage her in "battle." Not the war of the sexes but the lively competition of mind against mind. It is incredible how incisive the Scorpio woman can be in her arguments, and it comes as a surprise to many who have only observed her gorgeously sexy exterior. In giving her pleasure, remember her mind as well as her body; no one demands a more intelligent lover than the female Scorpio. That applies to the gifts you give her as well; alongside that bottle of dusky perfume under the Christmas tree be sure you have several books that show you are interested in *her* interests.

Monday, April 16: MOON IN SCORPIO. The week starts off with some real activity, and you may have to change the plans you had made in order to plunge into something new. It's both exciting and profitable, and you are able to take advantage of every moment. Some of those moments are spent in a fascinating encounter with a fascinating individual—possibly of the opposite sex.

Tuesday, April 17: You are on top of the world today, and on top of the situation. You may be called upon to play diplomat in a family or office dispute. The force of your personality makes it easy to solve the problem because both sides listen to you.

Wednesday, April 18: Watch out! Someone approaches with a scheme that could leave you out in the cold. Refuse to give up anything unless the return is worth it. Don't let yourself be fooled by your feelings about this person; he or she must be looked at just as coldly as anyone new.

Thursday, April 19: You are really pleased today when some work you did in the past pays off now. The rewards may not be monetary ones, but are good for the soul. You are proud to take on some new responsibility and aren't afraid of the pressure.

Friday, April 20: Dump what you no longer need, particularly a problem that really wasn't yours in the first place. You need lots of freedom now. Letting go of the past is not easy for you, but you have learned from experience that the results are usually positive. The lucky number is 9.

Saturday, April 21: You are feeling lots more independent today and lots happier for it. You are full of original ideas and eager to put them into action. Your willingness impresses others and they get on your bandwagon. Some of your new contacts are very good people to know.

Sunday, April 22: Trust the first feelings you get about a plan you hear of today. It may come from a relative or close friend you ordinarily trust, but it may not be wise to trust now—not because the person is insincere but because he or she is not very well informed.

Monday, April 23: For a while you have realized that things could be a lot roomier for you if you made some substantial changes. You may be smart to implement them now. Even in the planning stages you find the prospect of additional space very gratifying.

Tuesday, April 24: Get your act together right at the start today; there are some important details that must get your attention. When you have everything lined up you will be able to see the whole picture and feel a lot more secure about where you are going. The lucky number is 4.

Wednesday, April 25: You are red hot today and just can't seem to lose. Your bright aura is a real turn-on to a member of the opposite sex. Get involved, but only as involved as you can afford to be. You have a lot of fish to fry these days. The lucky number is 5.

Thursday, April 26: Yesterday's adventurous spirit carries over today—and so does the romantic mood. Indulge yourself because the pleasure principle is high on the list of do's today. There's always time to get back to reality tomorrow.

Friday, April 27: Watch it! Are you getting in too deep? Be sure you are listening with all your senses to what someone is saying. Not to worry, however; you rarely forget to protect yourself in emotional matters. Just know it is very important to do so now.

Saturday, April 28: You may have to revise your list of priorities today; something you didn't expect needs attention. It's a bit of a drag, but take heart. Later in the day you will get the chance to do what you want and show others how amusing you can be.

Sunday, April 29: Things go very quickly and smoothly today because you get a lot of help from your friends. As you work in a group, you get a chance to stimulate each other with new ideas. Some of them involve new ways you can keep fit with diet and nutrition.

Monday, April 30: You are finally able to cut the last tie with a past situation; it is a good feeling. You have done everything right so you know you are on firm legal ground. In fact, you may have even more rights in the situation than you are aware of. Be sure to double-check.

May 1984

Astronote to Scorpio: If you have ever observed that May is not your best month, you may be interested to know that there is an astrological reason. During the month of May the sun passes through the sign of Taurus, which is 180 degrees away from Scorpio in the great circle of the zodiac. That means the sun is literally shining on your opposite number and giving you rather short shrift. As a consequence, May can bring some particularly annoying frustrations to Scorpio—and that makes it the ideal time to examine how Scorpio deals with stress.

One of the blackest marks people give the sign of Scorpio is for holding grudges and seeking revenge. Sound a little familiar? In Scorpio's constant battle to win control over everyone and everything, the sign naturally runs into interference and opposition. After all, there are some other strong-minded people in the world too. Win, lose, or draw, Scorpio will never forget the confrontation. The proverbial "wounded Leo" is a pussycat compared with "scalded Scorpio." Scorpio has a supremely retentive memory and an incredibly vulnerable ego. Scorpio's sense of self is a great asset when it operates in a positive manner; however, self-confidence that is really runaway ego is nothing but a drawback. The image of the Scorpion is particularly apt for this sometimes self-destructive sign; the tail that lashes out to hurt others very often backlashes and wounds its owner. Scorpio's unfortunate tendency to take small setbacks in a big way starts in childhood. The Scorpio boy who doesn't make the team or the Scorpio girl who is left out of the club will harbor some pretty harsh thoughts about "the enemy" and may carry the bitter memory into adulthood. It is sometimes startling how long after the fact a Scorpio will bring up an unfortunate incident; "lighter" signs can only wonder at how devastated Scorpio feels and be amazed that he or she still remembers.

Tuesday, May 1: Make yourself as familiar as possible with the rules of the game. That way you will make a much better and fairer opponent. The situation requires a bit of delicate handling, however, so it might be wise to let the other side win at least one round.

Wednesday, May 2: New vistas open up and you can see a pretty clear road in front of you. As you prepare to make a new start, you may be startled to find that someone approaches you and wants to make it a joint venture. The involvement could be a good one, so seriously consider the offer.

Thursday, May 3: You have accepted the other person who wanted in and now you are sure you made the right move. Today you get another hunch and would do well to follow through on it. Your spirits get a big lift when someone you really like returns the compliment.

Friday, May 4: Today you get the real story on your new partner's financial standing, and it may be a little different than you anticipated. You can be of real help, however, and it benefits the two of you. Ask as many questions as you need in connection with the situation; shyness will only hold you back. The lucky number is 3.

Saturday, May 5: Take your eyes off your work for a while to look ahead into the future. Sometimes you get too close to the situation and can't see the forest for the trees. You will find an opportunity to open up the lines of communication with some people who can aid your cause. Take a creative approach to get closer to what you want.

Sunday, May 6: When you really look at things, you are able to revise your priorities according to your real values, and it is an almost spiritual experience. You are glad you can keep things in perspective and evaluate people according to their real worth rather than surface indications. An analytical person helps you see it.

Monday, May 7: You may feel like going for broke today when something catches your eye that you *must* have. It's a splurge to purchase it, but it is worth the money when everyone tells you how clever and generous you are. That makes a little sacrifice seem like nothing. The lucky number is 6.

Tuesday, May 8: Today you have some time to look at your current way of operating and see whether or not you can improve it. You can, and the new ideas you get will make things run a lot more efficiently. Someone close to you is really surprised at how capable you are.

Wednesday, May 9: This is one of those nitty-gritty days where the whole world seems to need your services. Grin and bear it. Look at it in a positive light: Isn't it comforting to know so many rely on you? Cold comfort, perhaps, but better days are coming. In fact, even today you get some good news about your health.

Thursday, May 10: At least today some others pitch in and help; it's great to know you have allies. These people share your concerns and understand your need for more working room. Perhaps with their help you can get it. Keep your eye on possible pitfalls that may escape you.

Friday, May 11: Your mind is a lot clearer than it has been and you are able to shrug off some doubts and fears that have been bugging you. You feel so good that you try to improve that for someone else who needs a lift—possibly someone confined to home or hospital. The lucky number is 1.

Saturday, May 12: You have a much better idea of where you are going and how you are going to get there. It's good to have your sense of direction back after its temporary absence. When you follow a hunch, you find it is possible to get into territory previously off limits and it is very revealing.

Sunday, May 13: MOON IN SCORPIO. This is the brightest day in a long while, no matter what the weather. You find you are very popular among people you thought were indifferent and you are relieved of some pressures. In fact, you are *so* popular you may find you are invited to a very intriguing social event.

Monday, May 14: It's great to be able to spot your own mistakes before anyone else does. When you see it, you correct it, even though it means a little backtracking; you know it puts you on much more solid ground. Your timing is terrific—but watch out for an ambitious person who may try to bump you.

Tuesday, May 15: You continue riding high today; a change that comes about doesn't throw you. In fact, it stimulates you to even more creative endeavors. One clue to your excitement is your interaction with some very outgoing and verbal people; resolve to spend more time with them in the future.

Mid-month memo to Scorpio: When Scorpio looks inward he or she should also examine the plus factors that are at the Scorpio's fingertips. As with any sign, the characteristics attributed to it are there for the taking, though the person can choose whether or not to incorporate them into his or her personality.

Scorpio's most potent ace in the hole is the sign's capacity for endurance. The legendary Scorpio willpower is a reality, and an important component of this complex personality. Nobody but nobody can outwait a Scorpio. By sheer grit, he or she will still be "hanging

125

on to the bone" when others decide to give up and quit. Scorpio's brand of patience is a lot more active than that of gentle Taurus, however. Scorpio not only endures, but continually puts more and more pressure on the other side. In fact, Scorpio can wear you out with constant grinding of the same old axe. It is a trait that should not be underestimated—either by the opposition or by Scorpio him-or herself. In times of real trouble, it is the Scorpio who is most able to keep his or her cool and never waver for an instant.

Wednesday, May 16: Accept a gift that says "I'm sorry" with as much grace as you can muster. You may very well feel like saying "I told you so," but you know how devastated that will make the person feel. Your kindness comes back to you when the whole thing is smoothed over and you are back in synch with him or her.

Thursday, May 17: Don't underrate yourself today. You have as much to contribute if not more than your competitors. If you take a positive approach, you'll be able not only to protect the assets you have but also to see an opportunity to increase them. The lucky number is 7.

Friday, May 18: You see what can happen? Just yesterday you thought you had bombed out but today you turn out to be the winner. The quick change in direction comes via the phone or mail, so check both sources of message. You still have someone strong who is not pleased with your progress, but you can handle him or her. The lucky number is 8.

Saturday, May 19: Use your dramatic ability to get your message over loud and clear today. You will make the kind of impression you want and demonstrate that a burden you have is really not yours to bear. What you say bears fruit as you realize people are listening to you and reacting.

Sunday, May 20: You may be feeling a little cocky about your recent victories; don't get carried away and get too independent. Someone may make it all too obvious that you are not alone in the world and that others deserve their fair share too. When you show understanding, the home-front atmosphere gets a lot lighter.

Monday, May 21: It's a time to be very canny about ways to improve your security. Some moves may have to be made now to ensure future benefits. You have the stamina and stick-to-itiveness to do some real studying that has to be done, but you know it is worth it. The lucky number is 2.

Tuesday, May 22: Today you can be "the most popular kid on the block." It may even surprise you when you are approached about some events to put on your social calendar. The whole day you are aware that you have greater freedom now and that some restrictions on your movements have been lifted.

Wednesday, May 23: You feel very drawn to someone of the opposite sex—he or she may even share your sun sign. Both of you feel the attraction and are tempted to act on impulse. It's wise to let the feelings sink in for a while before you let things get too serious. The lucky number is 4.

Thursday, May 24: Keep a pencil handy today to jot down some really great ideas that come into your head. It's a highly creative day. Younger people may play a big part in the day's activities and may also be the source of your inspirations. It's good to feel so stimulated and out of the doldrums.

Friday, May 25: Today you find you can be creative about some pretty basic things that need to be done. You figure out how you can cut the time needed in half! Good for you; take the rest of the day off and devote some time to personal renewal—particularly in the area of health and beauty.

Saturday, May 26: You are very impressed when someone whose sales ability you have long admired indicates that he or she wants to be an ally. Together you make a great team! The best part is that you are able to knock off a long-neglected task in record time.

Sunday, May 27: The green light goes on and it's full speed ahead for a pet project of yours. You have been waiting for this chance to show your stuff. It's a unique opportunity to impress others with your cleverness and diligence. The lucky number is 8.

Monday, May 28: Don't start anything new until you get something out of the way. You have a lot of bright ideas now, but if you play hopscotch you will never get what you want out of them. Look into your real rights in a situation that's a bit tricky. If necessary, get down to basics with someone who is involved.

Tuesday, May 29: Off you go into the wild blue yonder! You are leaving something or someone behind, but you have few regrets. It's exhilarating to realize you are going in a whole new direction. You even have your opposition spell it out for you; when you know what the competition is thinking, it's a lot easier to score.

Wednesday, May 30: Don't get thrown off the track by a conflict of interest on your part. A good look at your priorities will show you that the familiar course is the best one right now. It is also the one that is best for family harmony, and will please friends as well. The lucky number is 2.

Thursday, May 31: Financial matters may occupy you today; do the homework you must to ensure your chances of getting the backing you need. If you prove that you are stable and competent, it will be a lot easier to get what you want. Some people may try to divert your mind to pleasure, and a little bit is certainly indicated. You deserve a break!

June 1984

Astronote to Scorpio: It's the Scorpio male who's up for review this month—the one in which men have their special day. As husband and father, the Scorpio man is hardly your run-of-the-mill guy. The woman who decides to marry Scorpio may feel that it is her choice, but in effect she has become her mate's property. As possessive as the Scorpio husband is, however, there is a flip side to the situation. He will treat his wife as if she were a very prized possession, sparing nothing to keep her properly. If that sounds like some kind of slavery, you had better consult with the Scorpio's wife; she probably loves it. Even if she is quite competent herself, she will enjoy the feeling of security she gets from her attentive and considerate man. And though she may not talk about it, that smug smile will tell you he's a pretty terrific lover as well.

However, life with the Scorpio male is far from a bed of roses. The wife will have to learn to live with his occasional black looks (which are rarely meant for her), his bouts of emotional intensity which can be frightening, and his insistence that his household be run like a very tight ship. At times the Scorpio male is capable of real cruelty, even toward those he loves very much. It is a kind of perversity that they will just have to learn to put up with—as long as it doesn't happen too often. And—most frustrating of all to his spouse—the Scorpio man can be impossible to fathom at times. You may never learn what the mystery was, however, even if it preoccupied him for days.

Children raised by a Scorpio often have to work out their mixed emotions on the psychiatrist's couch later in life. They will complain that while daddy had his good moods and occasionally liked to play, most of the time he was a stern and demanding presence—even when he was totally out of sight.

A Scorpio father is indeed a mixed blessing: he tends to raise children with a deep-seated sense of responsibility, because he insists on devotion to duty. However, those same children may grow up with a permanent hate for authority figures. At best, the Scorpio's children will admire him for his strength and try to imitate it. Properly internalized, such a characteristic will prove a great bulwark against the storms they will have to weather in their own lives.

Friday, June 1: Use your powers of concentration to stick with a long-range project that must be planned for now. A romantic fling may be a tempting diversion and you will probably allow yourself to be diverted. A charming companion is hard to resist, even if he or she is a bit vain for your taste.

Saturday, June 2: Travel seems to be on everyone's mind today and it's a good time to see if the family is "in synch" about vacation plans. Get some additional information about where people would like to go and try to combine a trip with some educational projects.

Sunday, June 3: Sometimes it's hard for you to keep your mind off your work, whatever it is. Even at a social event you are on the lookout for people who share your interest and can be of help. Today you meet the kind of person you like, and it makes an outing worthwhile to you.

Monday, June 4: You know you have to get down to brass tacks today and put some solid structure under a project that needs it. When you check everything out, you discover that there were some loopholes; don't get mad, but be sure to reprimand the person responsible. The lucky number is 4.

Tuesday, June 5: Your best bet today is to get it on paper. If you try to articulate your problem without outlining it first, you will not be able to get the cooperation you need and want. Later on, accept an invitation and get in the party spirit; you need it at this time.

Wednesday, June 6: It's pleasant to start out the day knowing somebody loves you; a gesture of affection you receive puts you in a great mood. It will last throughout the day as things start moving in an upward direction. Even a minor adjustment you have to make won't throw you.

Thursday, June 7: You know you have been suspicious of someone's motives, so don't be a bit surprised when you find out the truth. It may teach you not to be so blind the next time. Don't let it get you down.

Friday, June 8: Today you are feeling a bit more rational about recent events and even are willing to involve yourself in someone else's dispute. It is important to state clearly at the outset what your terms are and that you don't want to have it take all day. Someone who shares an interest also shares a thought with you today.

Saturday, June 9: Don't be afraid to reach for the sky. Just because you were involved in a losing proposition doesn't mean you can't win the next time. Get in there and fight, but be very careful to protect what's valuable to you. Someone may be trying to get something for nothing.

Sunday, June 10: MOON IN SCORPIO. There you go! Now you see how easy it is to take the reins when you feel confident. It's great to get your energy back and to be able to trust your judgment. A very special person wants to go along with you in a very special project. Go ahead—as long as you get the chance to show your own good style.

Monday, June 11: You feel ready to take on the world today; satisfy yourself with just your little part of it. You almost can't make a wrong move now. A personal appearance of yours makes a great impression. You get a lot of satisfaction by teaching others what you know best. It is a form of learning for you.

Tuesday, June 12: Don't sell yourself short. There are a number of ways you can choose from to extend yourself now; be as selective as you want to be and ask for all the facts in each case. You will find that even the looking process is a source of good information.

Wednesday, June 13: Something pays off, to your great surprise. You never thought you would see any profit coming from that direction. Enjoy your windfall, but don't indulge in anything you have sworn off. The lucky number is 4.

Thursday, June 14: You feel a lot like getting around today and you do. It's almost impossible to keep up with you as you make your rounds. Don't get thrown off by a surprise visitor who causes you to change your plans. In such a sociable mood you will be most likely delighted to see him or her.

Friday, June 15: Someone seems to be talking in circles today; it's up to you to make him or her focus in on the main point. It's possible there's a subject this person wants to avoid; be sensitive to the fact and do not bring it up unless absolutely necessary. Be gentle and receptive.

Mid-month memo to Scorpio: If the Scorpio father sounds like some kind of monster, that is far from the truth. Since intensity is part and parcel of the Scorpio personality, he will be intensely interested in his children, and determined to give them the best of everything. In fact, it is the Scorpio father who can sometimes be accused of overindulging his brood. It will all be in what he sees as their best interests, however. For instance, if he is sports-minded (as Scorpio males often are) he will shower his boys with equipment and lessons—for the sport of *his* choice. And woe to the boy-child who has no athletic ability.

As for girls, it is not surprising that the Scorpio father will dote on them and encourage their femininity from an early age. The ironic part is that when dating begins, there is no more outraged father than Scorpio. His little girl going out with *boys?* The wife of the Scorpio male will have the additional burden of getting around daddy on behalf of her children. Though they are loved and adored by their father, they are not totally understood.

Saturday, June 16: You don't have to grab the first thing you see; you can afford to play the waiting game and shop around for a while. Why not get a professional opinion on what the wisest plan would be and purchase accordingly? The lucky number is 7.

Sunday, June 17: You are in for a bit of a surprise today when someone gives you a very good tip; you thought it was going to be a boring conversation. The benefit of experience can't be underestimated. You will discover that when you put your new information to work. The lucky number is 8.

Monday, June 18: It pays to be nice; today someone returns a favor that you had almost forgotten. It's a bright spot in an otherwise humdrum day. Though you are a little bored, realize that your activities are not only necessary, but vital to your security. Others will appreciate you.

Tuesday, June 19: It's possible you are right on the threshold of a very exciting adventure. Look into everything concerning this travel opportunity. It also is an excellent educational opportunity and could be rationalized that way so you can find room in the budget.

Wednesday, June 20: Watch your emotional responses today; you are particularly vulnerable now. Enjoy a romantic interlude but recognize it for what it is so you will not be hurt. It is flattering to have someone say he or she cares so much, but it would not be wise to bank on long-term involvement.

Thursday, June 21: Pay some attention to yourself today; you have been neglecting some responsibilities like medical and dental appointments. No one ever got points for sacrificing these things. It is in your best interests to do what is necessary to control weight, diet, health.

Friday, June 22: Today you run into someone who is just as much of a stone-head as you are—and has just as many ideas. With him or her you are able to work out a lot of details about a mutual job assignment. It's a case of either love or hate at first sight, but don't let your emotions about your new "partner" obscure your view of the opportunities available.

Saturday, June 23: Don't let anyone get away with easy answers today; demand the truth and the whole truth. Don't scare someone half to death in the process, however. Remember that it is hardly a life or death matter. You may be just amusing yourself and trying to stave off boredom. That isn't fair to the other person.

Sunday, June 24: Keep a tight rein on your tongue again today; diplomacy will get you much farther than threats and harsh words. One of your most important relationships is involved and it's not a good idea to be overly critical or emotional in your demands. The lucky number is 6.

Monday, June 25: You can really get down to business with someone who wants to work with you. Let him or her know just what your terms are, since there's no point in having something come up later that wasn't dealt with at the beginning. The legal aspects may prove a puzzle and you may need some outside help. After all, since this is going to be permanent you shouldn't leave a stone unturned.

Tuesday, June 26: People generally trust your judgment—particularly in money matters. It is not always infallible, but you give off an air of knowing what you are doing. Do not take it lightly, therefore, when someone asks for advice. Bone up on the subject of the inquiry and give as complete an answer as you can. It may benefit you, too.

Wednesday, June 27: You discover it's not as easy as you thought it was to get straight and complete answers to what you need to know. Keep on digging and don't give up the search. In the meantime, a relationship is getting a lot steadier and a lot stronger. It's the kind of thing that makes you feel very secure. Don't blow it.

Thursday, June 28: All your work the past few days has made it evident that you have to get some new systems going. Take time today to work them out. It will make you feel as if you have made a whole new start; you just about have! The lucky number you could try today is 1.

Friday, June 29: A family discussion leads to the subject of travel, which has been very much on your mind, too. The intimate chat gives you a warm glow and makes you realize that what is most important to you is pleasing those you love. You are released from some recent unworthy feelings and get a real uplift that feels almost spiritual.

Saturday, June 30: You are a political animal, and you know it. Nothing pleases you more than to make the rounds and give everyone a pat on the back. It ensures your popularity among the people who are most important to you. Another glad-hander rivals your style. A call from someone at a distance clarifies a confusing situation.

July 1984

Astronote to Scorpio: It's time to introduce another vital part of your astrological profile—your rising sign. Your rising sign—or ascendant, as it is sometimes called—is determined by the time of day you were born. If you know that time within an hour or so, you can find out what your rising sign is by looking it up in the chart on pages 69–70. What your rising sign does for you is provide a kind of cover for your sun sign (in your case, your sun sign is Scorpio). As your sun sign determines the real you in terms of what you want and how you go after it, the rising sign points to the way you come off to the world. Here's how the sign of Scorpio appears when it is masked by the various rising signs:

Scorpio sun sign with Aries rising You could have a real sting. Aries is often not very diplomatic and Scorpio can be very critical. Put them together and you get someone other people may try to avoid.

Scorpio sun sign with Taurus rising It is possible that you are highly sexual and that you telegraph that fact by your outward appearance and demeanor. You may attract more admirers than you can handle.

136

Scorpio sun sign with Gemini rising Where is that Scorpio reserve? Hardly in evidence at all when Gemini is the rising sign. You will seem a lot more approachable than you really are.

Scorpio sun sign with Cancer rising You could get the reputation for being a supersensitive type that needs special handling. Try to be a little more laid back.

Scorpio sun sign with Leo rising: What a dynamo! You come on strong and stay that way. Your exterior warmth is a little deceiving, however.

Scorpio sun sign with Virgo rising: You could strike people as a bit of a sour puss. Develop some genial come-ons for your public personality.

Scorpio sun sign with Libra rising You can be quite intimidating, but it serves you very well most of the time. People are impressed before you even say a word.

Scorpio sun sign with Sagittarius rising Your hail-fellow-well-met approach makes you instantly welcome. Your serious nature, though a surprise, is all the more interesting.

Scorpio sun sign with Capricorn rising Chances are you come off like a snob a great deal of the time. Try to warm up a little to take the "chill" off things.

Scorpio sun sign with Aquarius rising This is a great public appearance personality: someone who lives up to the interesting promise of his or her appearance.

Scorpio sun sign with Pisces rising You could easily be mistaken for a softy. This is an excellent disguise and one you should be aware of.

Sunday, July 1: You are tempted to believe everyone because a few people bring you messages that show you have increased your prestige. Take the compliments, but don't gloat. A little bit of humility would serve you well. It shouldn't be forgotten that you almost lost this cause.

Monday, July 2: You are gifted with a special assignment today that could involve travel. You aren't quite sure if you really like the extra demands on your time. Decide whether you want to continue going in this direction—because this kind of thing will happen more often from now on. The lucky number is 3.

Tuesday, July 3: It's a relief to be among some very different types today; you have gotten a bit jaded with your circle. When you see just how stimulating new contacts can be, you resolve to revise your life-style—at least in the area of your social life.

Wednesday, July 4: It is a particularly active holiday for you this year; you are celebrating more than a national milestone. You yourself get to a new level of agreement with someone of the opposite sex, and you realize this is an important change. The lucky number today is 5.

Thursday, July 5: Your instinct tells you not to "cast the first stone" in a family disagreement; your record is hardly spotless. However, you are brought to the brink of reconciliation by a gesture from someone who expresses gratitude for something you have done. Be a big person and get things going smoothly again.

Friday, July 6: Don't fool yourself; you can see very well what is really going on. You would rather have it otherwise, but there's no denying the situation. The only thing you can do to protect yourself is to define your terms very clearly and insist that they be adhered to. The lucky number is 7.

Saturday, July 7: MOON IN SCORPIO. Prepare to take some bows as the moon in your sign makes you particularly able to express yourself in a dramatic manner. You have the edge today, but don't abuse it. It's enough to know you are on solid ground and that others can't touch you. Your timing is excellent and someone is very impressed with your "love-style."

Sunday, July 8: It's up, up and away for you today! Something that's been standing in your way is almost miraculously removed and you are able to move forward much more quickly than you thought. Your circle is widening and there are some excellent contacts there for the making.

Monday, July 9: Be direct in all your dealings today; a forthright approach will yield results. The more personal your approach the better off you will be. Dress up a little and strut your stuff; it will be noticed and appreciated today. A couple of other strong minds like yours are fun to "spar" with today.

Tuesday, July 10: Your business acumen is especially good today; analyze some facts and figures to decide what tack you and some people who count on you should take. What you do for a family member is returned when that person helps; you resolve a knotty personal problem.

Wednesday, July 11: It's great to feel enthusiastic again; it's hard to remember ever being bored, but admit that you have been recently. It will help you recognize your need for more stimulation than the average. A social occasion fills the bill this time. What will you want next?

Thursday, July 12: You are getting around to finishing up a fairly long-standing project. A real goer—possibly an Aries—gives you the push that makes the difference. In the bargain you gain a valuable ally. Do whatever he or she says to finish this thing off; you will be getting very good advice.

Friday, July 13: A bell rings in your head today and you know you have the answer. One of the few things you usually trust is your intuition, and you are wise to do so today. Be sure to record your thoughts in writing so they won't escape you. Don't hesitate to fulfill the request of someone in your family circle; it's really not such a big deal.

Saturday, July 14: Stick close to homebase today; there's a lot that needs doing. You will find it soothing to your possibly jangled nerves to deal with a mechanical problem that needs attention. The basic things of life can make you feel secure if you put your mind to them and don't shrug them off as unimportant.

Sunday, July 15: You are aware that there is more going on than meets the eye and you are determined to get the whole story. When you do, you realize that you had better have some other options open so that you can make a quick switch to another tack if it becomes necessary. Some pretty tricky people are in the picture.

Mid-month memo to Scorpio: Whatever your rising sign, if you are a Scorpio you have a deep down belief in magic. This is often surprising to the Scorpio who has never even tried to do the old card up the sleeve routine. That is not this kind of magic that fascinates Scorpio, but the much more mysterious and sometimes "blacker" kind. Magic really is a belief or desire to and eventually an ability to control the forces of nature. Without jumping to the conclusion that Scorpio will really resort to black magic to attain his or her goals, it is legitimate to point out that many a Scorpio is a would-be sorcerer. Scorpio often really believes that his or her power can move mountains. The fact that it often does is not "magic" but an indication of the effectiveness of self-confidence and a well-honed ego. There are, of course, many Scorpios who will say they don't have an ounce of the stuff. These are the people who should be encouraged to get into their power and see the wonders it can work for them.

Monday, July 16: Your financial pressures are a bit lessened right now as your cash flows a little more freely. It gives you the latitude and the inclination to turn your attention to more creative matters, including relationships with the opposite sex. Someone may be trying to move in on you. The lucky number is 8.

Tuesday, July 17: Out of the mouths of babes can sometimes come great wisdom; today a young person startles you with his or her perceptions. The compliment you receive is particularly gratifying because you know it is sincere. It gives you a big shot of adrenalin, and you are glad to find your senses operating on all cylinders again.

Wednesday, July 18: You can freely express your independence today and be direct with other people. Whatever your activities, you are able to make them your own and people will remark at your special style. Some people who share your sentiments are great companions.

Thursday, July 19: It's necessary to deal with some pretty down-to-earth things today but you are up to it. The practical matters that concern you may include health checkups for you and your own. It's important to keep current with these kinds of obligations for your own sense of well-being.

Friday, July 20: Once again you must deal with the needs of dependents; the scenario may even include the basic care of pets! Your willingness to play "big daddy" or "big mommy" endears you to your co-workers who know you as someone not quite so soft and giving.

Saturday, July 21: Too much haste could cost you money; slow down and examine all the pros and cons of the situation before plunging in. The more you observe what others do, the better off you will be. You do not particularly like to play "follower" but this time it is just plain good sense.

Sunday, July 22: Spend a quiet day mulling over the week's events and preparing yourself for the week to come. A quiet talk with a very special person will help you get your perspective back and make you feel like facing the world again. The lucky number today is 5.

Monday, July 23: You feel quite close to home and family now and you accommodate them with a gesture of willingness to cooperate. They appreciate it and harmony reigns all around. Some understanding people help to make it come about.

Tuesday, July 24: You almost can't believe it, but someone gives you a second chance to prove your point. This time you do it so well you get double the return you would have in the first place. You should feel in an up mood, but don't let it make you be unrealistic about someone you should look at with clear vision. The lucky number is 7.

Wednesday, July 25: When you want to you can be a real organizer. That happens today and someone is so impressed he or she decides to give you a little more responsibility to handle. It should please you because it means before long you will make the jump into another bracket. Scorpio learns quickly that persistence pays off.

Thursday, July 26: Yesterday's victory allows you to let your mind wander into the future today. The dreams you dream are not impossible ones; in fact, they may be closer than you think. A lot depends upon getting your

142

priorities straight and deciding what is really most important to you.

Friday, July 27: The sorting out of priorities you did yesterday sets you in a new direction today, and it proves very productive. You see what you want and you are determined to go for it. You have all the wherewithal, and that's all you need.

Saturday, July 28: You can't neglect those closest to you and/or your own basic security. No matter how exciting future plans are, there are things that need doing right here at home. The diligence you exhibit in these matters gets you the attention of some people who are in a good position to help you later on.

Sunday, July 29: You realize how much you need a change of pace when you get it at a social affair you attend today. Among the many contacts you make is a highly creative individual who makes you see the potential of your own ideas. Keep up the relationship; it will be good for you.

Monday, July 30: Your inspiration of yesterday makes you get down to business even more quickly today. You see the necessity to work harder on something before exposing it to others. As you give it your attention today, note how easily ideas come to you; you have a lot going for you at this time—both personally and astrologically.

Tuesday, July 31: It seems as if your wishes can come true today; in fact, one of them does. Your friends are very encouraging about your future prospects and it gives you the kind of lift you need. It's good to have people believe in you, and some particularly interesting people tell you how much they do believe. The lucky number is 5.

August 1984

Astronote to Scorpio: One of the laws of the cosmos as seen by astrologers and occultists is that there are connections and correlations among everything in the universe. They see each zodiacal sign as ruled by one of the planets, and that the sign gets a lot of its individuality from the character of that planet. Scorpio's ruler is the planet Pluto, the most recent discovery in the heavens, sighted first in 1930. Aha!, thinks the skeptic, who was calling the shots before Pluto? How come Pluto fits so nicely into the plan? Who's kidding whom?

No one, least of all the astrologer. From ancient times, Scorpio's ruler was the passionate, hot-tempered Mars; yet even the earliest astrologers knew that a "higher form" of Mars lurked somewhere in the sky. At Pluto's discovery, the dense, powerful planet was immediately seen as a new form of the procreative energy Mars represents. Sex is connected with the sign Scorpio, and with both Mars and Pluto. The difference is that less-complicated Mars represents the sex *act* while to Pluto belongs the much more profound process of actual procreation. Does that mean Scorpios are more complicated than Aries people (who are ruled by Mars alone)? Yes, as a matter of fact they are.

And what of the legendary "force" of Scorpio? That is symbolically represented by Pluto more so than by Mars. Mars/Aries is an explosion of several tons of dynamite; Scorpio's power is likened to that of a thermonuclear reaction. Pluto—and Scorpio—can change the very atomic structure of things.

Wednesday, August 1: You find you are able to express yourself easily today; perhaps it's because you have been able to erase some nagging doubts and fears from your mind. Enjoy the new feeling of freedom and the

144

chance it gives you to breathe more deeply. A good friend calls in a vote of confidence.

Thursday, August 2: If you feel slightly hemmed in today, don't let it bother you too much. The delay is only temporary; you will be on your way soon enough. Use the time to begin to rebuild an old idea. This time, change your approach. The lucky number is 4.

Friday, August 3: MOON IN SCORPIO. The pace picks up so much it could leave you breathless; it would help if you readied yourself for anything. One possibility is being a star when you are asked to make up personal appearance. Don't let it throw you, and know that your timing is almost faultless now.

Saturday, August 4: You are able to take the reins today, wherever you are. In the domestic sphere your influence holds sway, and you may be the one to suggest a major purchase. Don't be afraid to do so; you know what you are doing now.

Sunday, August 5: You find you must make some rather untypical requests of household members now; let them know that you are turning over a whole new leaf and that they would do well to cooperate. Be very scrupulous in your accounting methods so that you don't accuse anyone unjustly. Make it clear that new measures are needed, however. The lucky number is 7.

Monday, August 6: You can wield your power without fear today; you are absolutely on target and will not mess up. You can take a lot of pressure and responsibility. Don't neglect a relationship, however; it's getting more intense than you ever thought it would.

Tuesday, August 7: Plunge into work today secure in the knowledge that what you need will be at hand. Not only can you get all the information you need; you locate something you thought was missing in the bargain. A person who seems a little pushy really has your best interests at heart.

Wednesday, August 8: You are in the mood for some new challenges and some new ideas, and both come your way today. You are able to display your new-found independence of thought by choosing among the many options and doing things *your* way. You may have to make a side trip, but what you gain out of it is worth the trouble.

Thursday, August 9: When you let yourself go and do not attempt to control your thought processes, you are capable of some fantastic intuitive leaps. You allow yourself one today and it brings you into much closer contact with the thing or person you desire. Your methods may not be totally orthodox, but you are on the right track at last.

Friday, August 10: It is important to pull yourself together today and resolve not to scatter your forces. A lot of interesting things beckon, but you must concentrate on those most important matters of security and property. Some good pals may try to divert you into more pleasurable channels, but make sure you get done what you have to do first.

Saturday, August 11: If you have built things on a solid foundation, they will withstand the testing that comes today. Actually it is you who is "on trial," and you acquit yourself well. However, you realize that some roadblocks will not disappear quite yet, and you must learn to live with them. The lucky number is 4.

Sunday, August 12: You know you have been feeling frazzled lately. You must confront the issue with someone close to you. Today the opportunity presents itself, and the discussion goes much more smoothly than you

146

thought it would. With accommodations on both sides you are able to work it out.

Monday, August 13: If you feel so inclined, throw your hat into the ring today; you have a good chance of winning. On the less purely pleasurable side, you may get some reminders of your resolutions about weight and other matters of health. Listen to someone who knows the ropes about how to discipline yourself and change habits.

Tuesday, August 14: You are inclined to be especially emotional today; keep your logic at the ready. It is important to strive for balance and avoid unnecessary risks. Listen to some people who know how to protect themselves in this kind of tempting situation.

Wednesday, August 15: When people come to you for advice and counsel today, be receptive and realize what a compliment it is to your good judgment. Those who rely on you regard you as a higher authority; it is both a burden and a blessing. Do what you can, but do not hesitate to say when you are beyond your depth.

Mid-month memo to Scorpio: Pluto is, of course, the legendary god of the underworld; since almost every early culture recognized such a place, Pluto changed his name from era to era. But, whatever his name, he has been inextricably bound up with the notion of death and transformation. What is most interesting about the ancient underworlds is that they were not final resting places. You went there to suffer a little and then enjoy a great and glorious rebirth. Pluto destroys but there is method in his madness; he wants to create anew.

Scorpio's ruler is obviously the reason why the sign is regarded as a "heavy"—and there is some truth in the description. However, often-misunderstood Scorpio should also be thought of as a lord over buried treasure.

Scorpio may use force to bring to light what is hidden—but what he finds there is often pure gold. This is the reason why so many Scorpios are involved with depth work—from oceanography to the more probing kinds of psychotherapy. Scorpio is also found in investigative work.

Thursday, August 16: Keep on plugging away at some tasks that need doing and you will get a pleasant surprise when someone recognizes your efforts. You didn't think anybody cared! It is even more gratifying that some co-workers who have been indifferent cooperate with you now.

Friday, August 17: You can't get away with doing things the same old way, so put your mind to work figuring out some new procedures that fit the new situation. You hate to get rid of anything, but in this case it is necessary in order to keep up with the progress that's going on around you. You don't want to be left behind, do you?

Saturday, August 18: Someone in your family circle is urging you to go out on a limb. Be gentle with him or her, but get the point across that it is *you* who is on the line. Naïve optimism is a pleasant thing to behold, but it can be counterproductive as well.

Sunday, August 19: What a perfect day to relax! Make the most of it by putting daily concerns totally out of your mind and forgetting about petty details and other annoying problems. You need the time for rest and recuperation; don't turn down a social invitation, however. The lucky number is 3.

Monday, August 20: Someone dumps a rather complicated matter in your lap and you realize that is a big responsibility. The first thing to do is familiarize yourself with all the basic rules and regulations. The subject is someone else's money and you must not take any chances; the important thing is to see what the future potential is.

Tuesday, August 21: There is more than a little bit of friction between you and a member of the opposite sex. It is important to open up the lines of communication and get a dialogue going. If both of you are absolutely clear about what makes the other tick, you can resolve your differences—even if you don't totally agree.

Wednesday, August 22: An adjustment in living arrangements satisfies both sides, and you are much happier as a result. Now you feel free to concentrate on long-range plans—some of which include travel. Think deeply about what is most important to you so you will make the right decisions.

Thursday, August 23: What a pleasant surprise! Something you thought you had blown is still possible. The secret is to be more creative than the next guy, which shouldn't be difficult for you. Someone is very jealous, however, and could try to sabotage your efforts. Watch it!

Friday, August 24: You are able to focus your energies today and as a result you get a great new opportunity to show just how effective you can be. Money is the possible prize here, and you decide to commit yourself totally to winning it. In the course of the day's activities you draw closer to someone who means a lot to you.

Saturday, August 25: If you have felt that you are beating your head against a stone wall, today the light dawns and you see it's all been for a good cause. You get a lot more prestige. Your new standing is in recognition of your achievements. Do you see now how important it was to persist?

Sunday, August 26: You are no longer confused about your aims; in fact, you feel positively enlightened now. One interesting result is that someone who was on the opposite side now wants to be on *your* side. Enjoy your moment of glory; it has more long-term ramifications than you realize now.

Monday, August 27: You can hardly believe it when someone you love announces his or her fondest desire— and it turns out to be yours as well. Together you will be able to make your wish come true. All it takes is a lot of guts and a little more persistence. You find you have other allies in your circle as well.

Tuesday, August 28: You plunge right into the day's activities, determined to make them pay off. The first thing you realize is that you must do more groundwork and get more information. You go to it, and find some fascinating new ways to move things along faster. Someone very clever is at your side to help.

Wednesday, August 29: Plan your moves carefully to rebuild things a bit more strongly. You don't want to find out that something needs revision later on. In a very roundabout way you learn a secret that is eye-opening; you put it to good use in terms of making your position more solid. The lucky number is 4.

Thursday, August 30: You are almost dizzy with the possibilities that present themselves today. There are so many options that you may feel baffled as you try to choose among them. Calm down and take them one at a time; a pattern will emerge quickly enough and you will see where you are headed.

Friday, August 31: You are faced with what seems like a momentous decision. Don't be intimidated. Let someone help you put things in perspective and you will see that what you do now is "set in stone." What is important is that you take the initiative and proceed with optimism.

September 1984

Astronote to Scorpio: If you are thinking about making a job change at the moment, it is not surprising. A kind of job-hunt fever strikes a lot of people at this time of year. Even if you are not in the market yet, it's instructive to look at your sun sign in terms of how well Scorpio is equipped for the world of work and career.

What works well for Scorpio on the job are the very things that often cause problems in Scorpio's private life. First of all, there is that passionate nature. What that translates into on the job is *interest and intensity*. Whoever hires a Scorpio must expect an employee who is going to get so passionately involved in the job that it is almost frightening. Especially to the boss who is not absolutely secure about his or her position. Scorpio is sometimes seen as a threat—even when Scorpio has no devious motives at all. Besides Scorpio's intensity, another reason someone of this sign is often suspect is that Scorpio is *so* secretive. Once again, poor Scorpio may be totally innocent, but the tendency to be close-mouthed is sometimes interpreted as deviousness. Try to be outgoing and friendly on the job.

Scorpio can be truly ambitious and quite ruthless in the business world. Give a Scorpio a goal and he or she will do anything to reach it. Once again, single-mindedness and the ability to concentrate are Scorpio's secret weapons. What is unfortunate is that Scorpio sometimes forgets his or her humanity in the process. Actually, in the contemporary business world, Scorpio's go-it-alone tendency is quite old-fashioned, and can prove counterproductive. Teamwork and management by participation are the buzz words today. Both the elitist and power-proud Scorpio boss are creatures of the past. It is to be hoped that the enlightened Scorpio, having a tremendous potential for success, will leave these images far behind.

Saturday, September 1: MOON IN SCORPIO. You did it! Congratulations! By doing things a new way, you turned the situation around and are now on top. Continue scoring points today as your sense of timing tells you exactly when to make the right move. The lucky number is 4.

Sunday, September 2: You can sit down to figure out where you stand financially with a lot of confidence now. The money picture looks pretty bright. You also get a nice "dividend" when a member of the opposite sex lets you know you are pretty great in his or her eyes.

Monday, September 3: With your financial feet on pretty firm ground, you are tempted to splurge on something rather expensive. You view it as an investment, as you should. As far as your family circle is concerned, you have done something wonderful for them. The lucky number is 6.

Tuesday, September 4: Set the record straight with some people who don't see it your way; it's up to you to be the realistic one. Let someone else get carried away and skate on thin ice. You know what you are doing and that is all that counts. Take a few minutes out to get in touch with a relative you haven't talked to in a while.

Wednesday, September 5: Someone gave you a tip yesterday that makes you connect with an interesting new source of information. The answers you get will make you look good to the higher-ups. Your ability to produce is noticed and appreciated.

Thursday, September 6: You are able to wrap something up today and it gives you a great sense of

152

accomplishment. You were able to negotiate easily, and it makes you realize how diplomatic you can be when you try. Someone older may need your help. The lucky number is 9.

Friday, September 7: You deserve a break today—and you get it in the form of some exciting and romantic dealings with a member of the opposite sex. It gives you the "new-start" feeling you need and your picture of things gets a lot brighter.

Saturday, September 8: You are right to feel your way through things today; your instinct about when to act is exactly right. In the course of it someone gives you some kudos that you consider long overdue. Accept the compliment graciously if you can.

Sunday, September 9: You are feeling rather mellow today and able to listen to some unusual ideas another family member has. It stimulates some creative thinking in you, and together you plan an exciting adventure or journey. The two of you draw closer as a result of the communication.

Monday, September 10: The adventurous spirit is still upon you and you feel the excitement of discovery. What you discover is an interesting opportunity. Some rather unusual people are the source of some rather unorthodox ideas that appeal to you now.

Tuesday, September 11: You come back down to earth and realize there are plenty of things right in your own backyard that need attention. It's a day devoted to nitty gritty tasks, but you get a sense of satisfaction when you get them over with. A good pal comes to your aid and offers a solution to a recent dilemma.

Wednesday, September 12: You have almost forgotten that someone owes you one and are pleased and surprised when he or she turns up today and returns the favor. It brightens a day that is otherwise not terribly exciting—except for a change of pace in your domestic sphere. You find your mate or partner wants you to try a little harder, and you agree to make an effort.

Thursday, September 13: You find you are able to zero right in on the problem today and knock it off quite easily and efficiently. The success of your technique makes you look around and see where it can also be applied. Some people are surprised when you turn up some jobs that had been almost forgotten. You get praise for your diligence.

Friday, September 14: It's ironic, but you were so successful at polishing things off yesterday that you get some additional responsibilities heaped on you today. You can handle it, and you should realize that you have been selling yourself short. It's nice when people notice.

Saturday, September 15: You will come out smelling like a rose if you control your urge to jump the gun. It's important to lie low and wait right now. The ball is in the other court and you should let the other party serve. Time is on your side. The lucky number is 9 today.

Mid-month memo to Scorpio: Scorpio is one of the true success signs by virtue of the willpower, strength, and analytical powers that are part and parcel of the Scorpio personality. These traits must be developed— but once they are there is no holding back. Here are some of the fields that Scorpio will find most suitable in his or her search for the right career:

The physical arts including gymnastics and dancing, death-related work, including counseling of the terminally ill and their families, mortuary management, and hospital administration; all investigative arts and trades, including exploration, research, and detective work;

154

diagnostic and healing arts, including surgery and intensive forms of psychotherapy; finance, taxes, and insurance, particularly life insurance, any and all jobs in the military-industrial complex; removal trades including sanitation and demolition; politics, all phases; research sciences, both organic and inorganic; religion, all phases including teaching and evangelical work; sex therapy; teaching, especially history.

Sunday, September 16: Don't beat around the bush today; come right out and say what you want. Show your independence and others will respect your point of view. You also have every right to ask for a complete and detailed account of what has gone on.

Monday, September 17: Your analytical mind is working at top speed today; it leads you to a possible way to increase your earnings. In another area you feel quite decisive and able to discuss where a relationship is going. Some important conclusions are reached.

Tuesday, September 18: A quick turnaround makes you the winner where you thought you were the loser. It all goes to show that it pays to advertise; people were observing your efforts after all. You find you like some rather talky types who used to annoy you. Open up and communicate!

Wednesday, September 19: Something that looked like it was an insurmountable obstacle just seems to fall away and you find it's clear sailing now. It puts you in an up mood and inspires you to do some long range planning for something you have wanted for quite a while.

Thursday, September 20: Your confidence comes back in spades and you find you are able to put yourself across in a way that impresses others. You are so impressive to a member of the opposite sex that he or she goes out of the way to compliment you. Some creative thinking you have been doing is put to work now.

Friday, September 21: Good thing you are feeling pretty strong now because a big challenge comes your way. You meet it easily—particularly because you are able to persuade others to cooperate. Nice going! Make a loving gesture to a family member by bringing home something he or she likes.

Saturday, September 22: It's possible your head has gotten a few sizes bigger lately with all the success you have had; today you have been taken down a peg. You will discover it's not a good idea to ignore advice from the top—even if you think you know more. The incident makes you look at your position more realistically.

Sunday, September 23: If you felt a little wounded yesterday, today you find out that a lot of people are on your side. One in particular offers you some good, sound advice. You begin to feel a lot more hopeful and even believe a wish *can* come true.

Monday, September 24: Your despondency vanishes totally today when you get a nice surprise, and something you have been carrying on your back is removed. Your much lighter frame of mind puts you in the mood for romance—and it does come your way.

Tuesday, September 25: The light dawns! That's what it was all about! What has been a deep, dark mystery now is perfectly clear. Now that you know, you see that it makes a lot of sense to join in a group endeavor you had dodged before.

Wednesday, September 26: Some very confidential information comes into your hands; exercise your strong willpower and do not reveal it. Private matters are very important to you, so you should respect that feeling in others. The owner of the material will be very grateful when you return it.

Thursday, September 27: MOON IN SCORPIO. You have that wonderful clear-headed feeling today. Some things that have been bothering you seem much less troublesome now. You also find that people want your company very much. Enjoy the popularity. You never know what can happen when you get out and get around.

Friday, September 28: You are feeling so up that it inspires you to offer your services to a charitable or community group. It is, of course, an altruistic gesture, but you are also aware that the people involved are both interesting and possibly valuable to know. You surprise everyone with your eloquence.

Saturday, September 29: It feels like you are being bombarded with messages and information today. Your recent mixing has brought you to the notice of some very active people. You feel like keeping up with them, and in the course of it you find the key to putting one of your pet plans into the works.

Sunday, September 30: It's a great day for a family reunion, and you find you have interests in common that you didn't know about. You exchange ideas about a hobby or mutual endeavor. You are actually uplifted by the experience and feel extremely peaceful. The lucky number is 6.

October 1984

Astronote to Scorpio: Earlier you found out that the planet Pluto rules the sign of Scorpio. Together Pluto and Scorpio rule a whole conglomerate of people, places, and things. It is most interesting and instructive to see

157

what some of them are—and amusing as well. They include:

Kidnapping; alibis; reptiles; autopsies; bandits; cemeteries; dictators; decadence; the genitals; power groups; the mob; Messina, Sicily; morticians; plagues; pornography; purification; Satan; atomic and subnuclear physicists; turning points; wizards; vampires; vice squads; Algeria; Dover; Halifax, Nova Scotia; Korea; Paraguay; Liverpool; magicians; vermilion; lumberjacks; heather; detectives; druggists; tax collectors; butchers; the Barbary Coast; floors; life insurance; researchers; rubbish.

Monday, October 1: You may be a little bit confused by a message that comes from someone who is difficult to reach. It may be necessary to read between the lines. By all means accept a social invitation that comes your way because it's an excellent way to make some new contacts—one of which will be very important in the future. The lucky number is 5.

Tuesday, October 2: Today you find a verbal sparring partner and the two of you go at it. You both enjoy the exchange, though in your case it's an opportunity to show how really witty you can be. The subject will not be momentous, but it does get settled to everyone's satisfaction.

Wednesday, October 3: You may feel like your thoughts are scattered today; you will have to use some self-discipline to zero in on what's important. Don't get carried away by your own self-delusions about someone or something. If you apply your good reasoning powers, you will see things as they really are and act accordingly.

Thursday, October 4: There is something you have been wanting to wind up, and you are able to do it today. You can give the word because now you have the authority. It's a bit of a drag to have to get involved in a messy situation, but when you get more responsibility, you get more problems, too.

Friday, October 5: What a relief to find out you are a lot better off than you thought; was it worth all the worrying? What you must concentrate on now is getting things done in order to consolidate your position. The lucky number is 9.

Saturday, October 6: Sometimes you are not too willing to experiment, but you find your recent risk pays off. It makes you feel very creative—and romantic, too. It's a fine day for a fling, so enjoy! In the course of it, you find you are able to come to a meeting of the minds with something you really care about.

Sunday, October 7: You seem to be the one picked out to deal with a problem that's bugging a young person. You should be flattered that he or she trusts you enough to come to you. As you analyze his or her problem, you find you get a lot out of the exercise yourself. Sometimes the best way to learn is by teaching.

Monday, October 8: There are a lot of good vibes in the air today and a feeling of excitement. A couple of interesting invitations may come your way and your social calendar may look pretty full. On top of it all, someone starts you thinking about a trip! Don't overload your schedule.

Tuesday, October 9: Never fear—that lost cause rears its head again and is very much alive. You get another chance to see it through to completion. Don't neglect some niggling details that have got to be taken care of. A lot of people are depending on you.

Wednesday, October 10: You never can tell who will end up being your best pal. Today you cement a relationship with someone and you begin to feel you are both working on the same team. He or she lets you in on some office gossip that starts you thinking. You could use a change of pace and this could be the ticket.

159

Thursday, October 11: Don't let anybody get to you today; you may be feeling a little hassled. If you take it slow and easy—and *refuse* to be backed into a corner—you will make it through fine. Tomorrow is time enough to be decisive. Let the others talk today.

Friday, October 12: Don't waste any tears on what has to be gotten rid of; you personally benefit by the new environment that grows out of the temporary chaos. Progress is always a little confusing at first. Be sure to do your homework on a proposal that's made to you, however.

Saturday, October 13: Someone you have an in with agrees to bend the rules a little today and you are the one who is favored. Say "thanks" and demonstrate it by being even more productive than usual. One of your relationships is undergoing a bit of a transformation, but you will like the result.

Sunday, October 14: It may be necessary to get a little rougher than you like with certain people who owe you an accounting. You have to demand the facts and all the facts. No one is trying to cheat here, but there is a bit of a coverup due to embarrassment. The lucky number is 9.

Monday, October 15: You are a big boy or girl now, so you shouldn't be afraid of a new situation that's a bit challenging. A new start is always good for the ego, and you could stand a little boost. There are a lot of people in there rooting for you, so you shouldn't have to worry about a thing.

Mid-month memo to Scorpio: Medical astrology—the art of diagnosing and treating illness via the horoscope—has a long and illustrious history. From earliest times certain parts of the body and their illnesses have been ascribed to certain combinations of planets and signs.

Here are the things the medical astrologer connects with Pluto/Scorpio:

Adenoids; appendicitis; excretory organs; genitals; kidney stones; the nose; all operations; peristalsis; pubic bone; reproductive system; ruptures; scurvy; venereal disease; the subconscious; the spleen; ulcers; pituitary gland; the pelvis; ileac region; the groin; the bladder.

The association of sex with the sign of Scorpio obviously derives in part from Scorpio's "rulership" over the genitals and the reproductive system. The passionate nature of Scorpio is real, however, and the sign's strong drives are often the cause of intense and extreme behavior. One will meet two types of Scorpios, however: those who frankly enjoy their sensual and sexual nature and those who deny it and sometimes act out their sexuality in less healthy ways.

Tuesday, October 16: The course is getting much steadier and you feel you have a handle on the situation. You get help from someone you once helped—it pays to be nice! You are dealing with some pretty tough customers now, but you can survive very well.

Wednesday, October 17: This starts out like an ordinary day but quickly changes into an exciting one. All of a sudden a million possibilities seem to present themselves, including a travel opportunity that's hard to resist. Don't resist it; you know it will do you a world of good and help you sort out what you really want out of life.

Thursday, October 18: You are not usually a nit-picker but today you discover you have to make a pest of yourself to make sure all those little things get done. You may hear some grumbling from others and you may not be radiantly happy either—but it's all necessary.

Friday, October 19: The time has come to have it out with a member of the opposite sex. The discussion needn't be a confrontation—but it is necessary to find out exactly what is on his or her mind. Try to be as cool and analytical as possible. In the meantime you will be delighted with a report card you get and it boosts your self-confidence.

Saturday, October 20: All is quiet on the domestic front and your nerves are calm. In this harmonious atmosphere, you are able to have some really productive discussions about fixing things up. Some congenial people are full of suggestions that you like. The lucky number is 6.

Sunday, October 21: This is turning out to be an even nicer weekend than you thought; there is nothing like a little confession to bring people closer together. That happens to you now with someone who is immensely appreciative of your understanding. The two of you get a lot of emotional fulfillment out of the incident.

Monday, October 22: You might have a rather severe case of the Monday blahs today, if not actually the blues. It's hard to get your mind off someone you know is tied down and suffering for it. Reach out to him or her—perhaps with a visit. You will feel a lot better.

Tuesday, October 23: It's nice to be appreciated, and today you can tell that you are. Your fame is spreading among those who know you as a good friend. It gives you a warm glow that you should store away for a chillier time. The lucky number is 9.

Wednesday, October 24: MOON IN SCORPIO. Oh, what a beautiful morning—for you, anyway. The moon in your sign fills you with vim and vigor, and gives you a special "something" that others find hard to resist. Seize the day and get your message across where it counts. You can easily get a jump on the competition.

Thursday, October 25: Everybody seems to want you today, and you have to make some choices. You can't please everybody, so please the most important person—you. It won't be taken as selfishness because in the long run everybody gets something out of it. Ignore the grumbling they do now.

Friday, October 26: Get your act together fast today. You are going to need some fast answers to some questions that will be fired at you. Your inquisitor is not hostile—just in a big hurry to get on with things. You can help a lot and make yourself look like a hero—especially when you locate something that everyone thought was lost.

Saturday, October 27: Don't get your back up when someone says, "Sorry, that won't do." If you look at it objectively, you know it can be done better. Take the minor setback gracefully, and resolve that it won't happen again. For some fun to lighten up the day, try number 4 for luck.

Sunday, October 28: You have a hot prospect right on the premises; don't let him or her get away before you make your pitch. The more directly you ask for what you need the more likely you are to get it. If nothing else, you will get someone interested enough to ask more questions. Get the backup of some fast-talking friends.

Monday, October 29: You can be a sheer genius sometimes at figuring out how to make do with what is at hand; someone applauds you for your talent today. A pleasant surprise comes your way in the form of a gift from out of nowhere. Enjoy your windfall.

Tuesday, October 30: You feel vaguely uneasy today and have trouble pinning down the cause: could it be that you have too many options? Toss some thoughts around with a few people who can be objective. Then zero in on the thing that gets the most votes. You won't feel quite so much at loose ends when you do. The lucky number is 7.

Wednesday, October 31: Though you don't really like to play the heavy, you may have to come down on some holiday pranksters who could get carried away. Fun is fun, but you have to know where to draw the line. You get backup from others who feel the same way.

November 1984

Astronote to Scorpio: Happy birthday month!—though many of you celebrate birthdays in October. People often wonder if it makes a difference what *part* of a sign you are born into. The answer is yes; each sign is broken into three basic segments.

If you were born from about October 23/24 to about November 3/4, you are what is known as a first-decanate Scorpio—born within the first ten days of the sign. You come under the direct rulership of the planet Pluto and therefore exhibit all of the Scorpio traits in their purest form. It is first-decanate Scorpios who tend to be the most intense, the most passionate and the most driven in terms of career. They also may be said to have the most solidly constructed egos and are therefore sensitive to indifference or opposition.

Scorpios born from November 4/5 to November 14/15 have the moon as a coruler along with Pluto. This is a considerable softening influence, and second decanate Scorpios are generally a lot more easy to deal with. They are unfortunately also less ambitious than the "pure" types of the first decanate, and sometimes find themselves standing still while others move ahead. However, the second decanate Scorpio has a lot simpler time of it finding the right mate. There is a sweetness that sometimes seems untypical of the sign, but that is intensely attractive to members of the opposite sex.

Born from November 14/15 through the end of the sign are those Scorpios who reflect the rulership of the planet Neptune as well as Pluto. Neptune is a bit vague and this means that third-decanate Scorpios can have a difficult time trying to figure out where to put their energies or how to use their considerable power. Because of it, third-decanate or "late" Scorpios can be said to be the most dangerous. Unfulfilled ambition or thwarted love can make a mighty unhappy Scorpio, and one who just might take it out on the other fellow.

Thursday, November 1: Today you bounce back and it feels good to feel great again. Throw yourself into the work at hand and you will cut through a lot of it. Some of your creative energy should go into trying to solve a security dilemma at home base. Someone there gives in on a major point and you are relieved.

Friday, November 2: Who says you don't have talent? Look at what you are able to turn out today. Of course, you have lots of inspiration that comes from some exciting creative types you meet. Take a chance on a far-out possibility that could possibly be romance.

Saturday, November 3: Don't act like a know-it-all when someone makes a gentle suggestion today; there's always something you can learn—especially from one who has experience. You may find it hard to keep your mind on your work, however, because a blossoming relationship demands equal time.

Sunday, November 4: Someone with a lot of spirit tries to get you in the mood for fun. It turns out to be a great play day—complete with children in the picture. On a more serious note, someone surprises you by asking your opinion; you feel flattered that he or she would think of asking you.

Monday, November 5: One look at what's ahead of you tells you there must be a better way. You find it and are able to polish off some routine business rather quickly. Your ability to cut through the red tape and zero in on the problem impresses even you. The lucky number today is 1.

Tuesday, November 6: Spend a little time on yourself today; you could use it. How long *has* it been since you saw your friendly dentist? A little voice tells you your suspicions about someone are correct, and you resolve not to be so gullible next time. If there is a next time.

Wednesday, November 7: Don't get stuck in the mud. There's a big, wide, wonderful world out there and it's just waiting for you. Make a mental breakthrough and see that your expectations could be a lot higher than they are. A good friend with lots of ideas could be inspirational to your thinking.

Thursday, November 8: You may come head to head with someone pretty tough today; but you can handle him or her. Agree to make some revisions, but hold the line on others. You may get a rather unusual request from a relative; try to fulfill it if you can. You know how much he or she trusts you.

Friday, November 9: It had to happen sooner or later; today's the day you and someone you care about have a long talk. You are the one who is able to be more analytical; try to keep emotions at a low temperature. There are things that must be done by both of you; the important thing to sort out is "who does what to whom."

Saturday, November 10: There are some questions you would rather not ask, but you must. No sense going in on something with someone who doesn't have the qualifications or abilities. You could get burned. Some other rather solid types will be asking questions too, so don't be shy. The lucky number is 6.

Sunday, November 11: A time bomb situation requires special handling; you know how sensitive a certain person is to criticism. You also know, however, that person can be dangerous if allowed to run amok. Play the diplomat, but don't get sucked in by a lot of sweet talk. Look at the thing with very open eyes.

Monday, November 12: Not just another Monday for you—things happen fast and furious. Try not to get overly rattled by the pace. You may have to dash off a quick note that you would rather spend more time on, but the important thing is to clear things off your desk as quickly as possible.

Tuesday, November 13: You are able to stay above the crowd today and see the larger picture. Refuse to get involved in petty jealousies because they are not worthy of you. What's right is right. You have an ally who also believes in fair play and a spirit of cooperation. The lucky number is 7.

Wednesday, November 14: Yesterday's events make you realize that there's more to life than work and worry. You focus on some lofty goals that include broadening your knowledge of something that is important to you. Some people who think like you could be very helpful in giving you some tips.

Thursday, November 15: Today you are determined not to get too embroiled in things. Together with some other determined individuals you come up with a new plan that allows everyone a lot more flexibility. It gives you a sense of satisfaction.

Mid-month memo to Scorpio: No matter what decanate a Scorpio is born in, he or she probably suffers from

167

inner tension. Living life at Scorpio's intense level leaves you prey to all the ills that are related to inner stress. That means that of all the signs, Scorpio is the one who should devote at least some time to strenuous physical activity. The only way for Scorpio to work out of an emotional bind is often to work out physically. The so-called "runner's high" could literally save the Scorpio who has gotten tied up in knots of frustration. Relaxation can be achieved in other ways, of course, and disciplines like meditation should not be ignored; but for the quickest and most lasting relief from stress Scorpio should put the body to work as diligently as the mind.

Friday, November 16: Your new start continues to unfold today. By keeping your options open for a while longer, you will be able to make the most of all opportunities. Your willingness to diversify is noted and given the nod by some rather prestigious people. You are on your way!

Saturday, November 17: Someone or something may interfere and threaten to divert you from your long-range plan. Stick to your guns. You have a lot more questions to ask and a lot more information to locate. Regard this only as a small detour not a major rerouting. The lucky number is 3.

Sunday, November 18: No matter how tempted you are to "blow your cool," it is important to prevent a minor flare-up from becoming a three-alarm fire. If people start to get too personal in their arguments, insist that they stick to the facts. It won't be easy because a couple of very imaginative people are involved.

Monday, November 19: Much to your surprise someone confides in you that he or she would not at all mind making some changes in the living arrangement—possibly even a major move. It requires a lot of thinking, so you shouldn't make a snap judgment. Listen.

Tuesday, November 20: My, isn't it nice to be so popular? There are a number of ways you can go, but it is important to be objective and figure out who is going to give you the best deal. You don't have to worry because you are in a pretty strong position. The lucky number is 7.

Wednesday, November 21: MOON IN SCORPIO. Go for it! You can't lose today as long as you keep your eye on the ball. If you spot an opportunity to pull a power play, feel confident that you can pull it off. Timing is very often a key to success, and your timing is great now.

Thursday, November 22: Your "moon high" means you continue to be on a roll today. If your natural sense of caution tells you when to go and when to stop, trust your judgment. A lot of people have their eye on you so it is important not to appear *too* confident. The lucky number is 9.

Friday, November 23: An investment opportunity looks very good. It may be a departure for you, but it's worth the gamble. You are in a particularly creative cycle and what you do now will bear fruit in the near future. That includes love, where a new start is indicated.

Saturday, November 24: Steady as she goes! Today is a day to clean up after the week's activities rather than to plunge into something brand new. Take the time to bask in the glow of the new recognition you are getting from others. Don't underestimate your assets.

Sunday, November 25: It's a pleasant day of comings and goings of friends and relatives. You may be doing some of the going. It reminds you how much you really enjoy catching up on what's going on with everyone. This time you have plenty to tell, too.

Monday, November 26: Security is very important to you, as it should be, and today something happens that adds to yours. You may very likely get a return on a recent investment—or have someone surprise you by repaying a debt you had almost forgotten.

Tuesday, November 27: Again today you find out that something you own is more valuable than you thought and your personal stock goes up. Your recent efforts put somebody very important in your corner. Keep on looking good. The lucky number is 5.

Wednesday, November 28: You are in a cycle where things of home and property assume a lot of importance. To shore up some assets, you should focus on a long-term project where you could renegotiate on better terms. Your family rallys round and everyone wants to be part of the act. It's a good idea.

Thursday, November 29: Now that you have a lot of busy work out of the way, you feel confident and able to turn your attention to new things. Your natural curiosity helps you solve a mystery and everyone gets a big laugh out of it. You are feeling a lot better too and are less worried about health.

Friday, November 30: Today you feel so good you want to tell the world. Keep it within your little circle, but do have fun with them. You get a bright idea and the gang decides to go along. Your enthusiasm could get *anyone* fired up. The scenario proves to be a lark for all involved and you are the star.

December 1984

Astronote to Scorpio: The "sun sign" game is fun to play—especially when it involves the famous. How many of the following would you have guessed were born under the sign of Scorpio?

Richard Burton; Chiang Kai-shek; Madame Curie; Charles de Gaulle; Billy Graham; Bill Sunday; Teddy Roosevelt; Jonas Salk; Katharine Hepburn; Charles Atlas; King Hussein; Goldie Hawn; Sally Field; Ghengis Khan; Kurt Vonnegut; Henry "The Fonz" Winkler; Burt Lancaster; General George Patton; Stan Musial; Charles Manson; Charles Bronson; Prince Charles; Rock Hudson; Johnny Carson; Grace Kelly; Robert Kennedy; Pablo Picasso; St. Augustine; General Erwin Rommel; John Keats.

Saturday, December 1: You are still in pretty high spirits, but you better look before you leap today, no matter how much you want to get going. If you are too impulsive you may regret it later on; play the old waiting game for now. To amuse yourself in the meantime, you find a young person is a delightful companion and an important new ally.

Sunday, December 2: The best place for you today is in the workshop, sewing room or with any hobby of your choice. As you practice your skills, go over the past few days in your mind and get your perspective back. You need it, plus a second wind. It's nice when someone arrives and says "I'm sorry" with a little gift.

Monday, December 3: You find you are able to cut your losses in one area and see potential gain in another. It makes you dream a little about the future. As a bonus, you get a nice nod of approval from someone it's important to impress. The lucky number is 9.

Tuesday, December 4: Are you secretive or are you just plain shy? Nobody knows for sure. Today you get up enough nerve to let some others see your real style, and they are impressed. It inspires you to think about being a lot more independent in your actions.

Wednesday, December 5: There is practically nothing that can't be solved by a little creative thinking. Something you do today results in an unusual solution to a problem that's been bugging others besides you. It's a public relations coup for you, and you get thanks from all sides.

Thursday, December 6: A little opposition shouldn't scare you; your views are as important as those of the other side. Stand back and get the wide-angle view for best results now; you can fill in the fine points another time. Get all the material you need at your fingertips— then make your attack! You may be surprised at how easy it is. The lucky number is 3.

Friday, December 7: A friend does some big talking— but don't believe what you hear. He or she is sincere, though, and doesn't mean to throw you off. However, you are realistic enough to know that results are way down the road. Don't get discouraged; get busy.

Saturday, December 8: What you learned yesterday makes you resolve to rely on yourself now. It's like getting pennies from heaven when you hear some good but surprising financial news. You and a loved one decide to get serious about a project that seemed like a dream not long ago—and the experience is good for both of you.

Sunday, December 9: How sweet it is! A whole day to relax with people you like, and it turns into a kind of reunion when someone unexpected arrives. Everybody is full of advice on how you can set your house in order and make it more beautiful. You know they all mean well, but you follow your own course.

Monday, December 10: Don't get bogged down today; it's too important for you to look ahead and do some advance planning. You know this isn't the way you want it all the time, and that there are some things you can change. The key is to know what you really want; discuss it with someone near and dear.

Tuesday, December 11: You have a pretty clear vision now, and they can't take that away from you. Someone who is rather narrow-minded annoys you—but can be successfully ignored. He or she will be sorry when you go on surging ahead. Act on your ideas.

Wednesday, December 12: Today it's down to business and some thoughts about how to improve it. You know you have to concentrate to improve your position—and your chance to get free. One practical move is to relieve yourself of a burden that shouldn't have been dumped on your shoulders in the first place.

Thursday, December 13: You are doing so well you stand in line for a big step forward. Is a promotion what you want—or do you want out? It's important to get a fix on where you want to go from here. The lucky number is 1.

Friday, December 14: With a little bit of luck and some help from a family member you are able to close a deal and it makes you feel a lot more secure. Now if only your other wishes would come true. They can if you continue on your forward course.

173

Saturday, December 15: You amaze yourself with the fabulous public performance you give today. You really are able to win friends and influence people. Though it's not something you consider one of your great strengths, it's a nice skill to have in your pocket for future reference.

Mid-month memo to Scorpio: The list of famous Scorpios is a fascinating one in terms of the extremism of the sign. There are a number of "saints" as well as a few outstanding "sinners," and the number of military types is striking. The Scorpio who embodies the intensity of the sign—especially in his physical aspect—was piercing-eyed, brilliant, and daring Pablo Picasso.

Sunday, December 16: It's fun to reminisce with someone older about the way times used to be. And it is instructive too. You find you have new respect for the person and for the sense of history he or she gives you. Some of what you learn is very applicable to your present situation. The lucky number is 4.

Monday, December 17: Months ago, who would have thought that the person you draw closer to today would ever be a friend? Office politics makes strange bedfellows. Together you are able to unravel a murky situation and find out what someone's motives really are. You form a united front for future action.

Tuesday, December 18: MOON IN SCORPIO. You bounce out of bed today full of ideas and energy. In addition to your high spirits, circumstances swing around and give you a shove in the right direction. You are able to pull off a few real bargains and love the way they look in your home. Your partner approves heartily.

Wednesday, December 19: You are in a take charge frame of mind again today and others really notice. There is no point in trying to push you around. It's a good feeling to be on top of things and to insist on the best from everyone. Accept no substitutes for the kind of quality you want.

Thursday, December 20: Today you put on your creative hat and find that a hobby you have been dabbling in could become the real thing and a source of profit. You are inspired to greater things when you find just the stuff you have been looking for to get the effect you want. Congratulations! You're in business.

Friday, December 21: It looks as if your enterprise can really take off; get yourself the right kind of manager now. It's important to know just what you have and how to make the most of it. Sure it's prestige, but you want some cold cash, too.

Saturday, December 22: The experiences of the week have left you with a satisfied feeling, but today more good things come into your life. One of them is a second chance to make a relationship work. You both want it, and since you both are intelligent adults, you should be able to work things out.

Sunday, December 23: The new start you have embarked on recently has brought you a lot of advice you didn't ask for. Today you get some from a well-meaning relative; be nice. You know very well how to protect your interests and are in no danger, so you can afford to look interested—and then do your own thing.

Monday, December 24: You find you have to do some coddling of someone who has felt neglected; do it and make sure everyone is "in synch" for the holiday. Everyone is diverted by a rather unusual gift that comes along and causes a lot of comment. The lucky number is 3.

Tuesday, December 25: This is one of the wildest holidays you have had in a long while! There is a lot of traffic in and out and more people drop in than you expected. It's all very pleasant activity, however, and later on you and your family do some quiet planning together for the year ahead.

Wednesday, December 26: You may be asked to be more generous with your time than you would like. Someone wants to get in on your creative act, but you know there is only room for one. Respond graciously, but let the person know firmly that you are in this alone. Some rather confusing messages arrive about some property you own.

Thursday, December 27: It's clean-up day as you get rid of holiday debris and put everything back to rights. It's a good time for a quiet talk with a young person who is close to you. He or she expresses feelings of love and you find it's the best thing that's happened all week.

Friday, December 28: The pace picks up again today and you find yourself running around quite a bit. Some unexpected events change your game plan for the day, but you find you enjoy the variety. You can't be too careful in looking over some kind of legal paper or contract; have you read everything?

Saturday, December 29: One look in the mirror tells you it's time to call a halt to holiday splurging. You decide to put a few New Year's resolutions into effect early. An older family member needs some attention and you should give it ungrudgingly—even though you would much rather be doing something else.

Sunday, December 30: You need a lot of concentrated effort to finish off a project that's been hanging around a while; today you get the inspiration and the energy. Later on you have a rare opportunity to talk with the whole family plus some others who like the same things you do.

Monday, December 31: It's a nice way to end up the year—quiet and peaceful, but with some stimulating companions. Together you all resolve to make next year an even better one. You personally feel you have made a lot of progress and that 1983 was in many ways a milestone year.

ABOUT THE AUTHOR

Born on August 5, 1926, in Philadelphia, Omarr was the only astrologer ever given full-time duty in the U.S. Army as an astrologer. He also is regarded as the most erudite astrologer of our time and the best-known, through his syndicated column (300 newspapers), and his radio and television programs (he is Merv Griffin's "resident astrologer"). Omarr has been called the most "knowledgeable astrologer since Evangeline Adams." His forecasts of Nixon's downfall, the end of World War II in mid-August of 1945, the assassination of John F. Kennedy, Roosevelt's election to a fourth term and his death in office . . . these and many others . . . are on record and quoted enough to be considered "legendary."

ABOUT THIS SERIES

This is one of a series of
Twelve Day-by-Day Astrological Guides
for the signs in 1984
by Sydney Omarr

SIGNET Books of Special Interest

To order use

coupon in front

of the book

How your Personal Horoscope can bring you wealth, love, success and happiness.

By Norman P. Kennedy

Did you know that you can have your personal natal horoscope cast and analyzed free? You can. The American Astrological Association, the largest known astrological society in the world, is conducting astrological research. They need birth information for this project. If you send them your birth data, they'll cast your horoscope on their computer, for research purposes. And, if you wish, they'll send you a copy of it.

Your personal natal horoscope will consist of 9 pages and 3,000 words. Your horoscope will analyze your strengths and weaknesses. It will tell you how to take fuller advantage of your talents, and show you how to overcome your weaknesses. Your horoscope will discuss your lovelife, tell you who you should be sexually compatible with, and outline your marriage potentials. It will also cover your marital and child relationships along with your health, your career opportunities, and finances.

Your personal computer horoscope will not be the general kind found in paperbacks. Your horoscope will analyze your sun-sign, moon-sign, rising-sign and planets according to your exact time, date, month, year and place of birth. Many people don't understand the importance of their moon-sign and rising-sign. Your moon-sign refers to your subconscious mind relating to your past. It also affects your childhood conditioning, instinctive patterns, feelings, and inner nature. Your rising-sign shows you how to project yourself. It is the mask you wear before others.

Your horoscope will be cast on the Association's gigantic 370—145 IBM computer. It contains over 24,000,000 bits of authenticated astrological information. No two horoscopes, produced by the computer, are ever alike.

Few people realize that the majority of famous people used horoscopes just like the ones produced by the Association to discover and cultivate their talents and thus gain success and riches. Nearly all successful people use astrologers — politicians, movie stars, businessmen, doctors and lawyers. Many famous scientists were astrologers themselves; such as Sir Isaac Newton, Carl Jung and Sigmund Freud. Famous business tycoon, J.P. Morgan, used astrology to achieve his wealth. He did not make a financial move without consulting his astrologer. Astrology helped the allies win World War II by predicting the enemy's moves. A horoscope of Adolph Hitler done on January 30, 1933, exactly predicted the course of World War II. Astrology was used to find and keep the successful marriage of Grace Kelly and Prince Rainier.

These rich and famous people are no different than you and me, except for one thing. They weren't forced to use the general astrology carried in paperbacks. They could afford to pay a professional astrologer hundreds of dollars to cast their horoscope from their exact time and place of birth. Now you too can have your personal natal horoscope cast from your exact time and place of birth.

Here's how it works. The A.A.A. will cast and analyze your natal horoscope. Since your horoscope has already been produced for research, you may get it for only a $3.00 charge plus 50¢ to cover postage, handling and the cost of making your duplicate copy. You get the expensive casting and analyzing process, which could cost $250, FREE.

If you would like to help us with our research and take advantage of this special offer by ordering natal horoscopes for yourself, for your family or for your friends, simply do this: Send me the name, address, time, month, day, year and place of birth for each person on a piece of paper along with the $3.00 copying cost and 50¢ postage in cash, check or money order for each horoscope. Make checks payable to American Astrological Association. (If you don't know your exact time of birth, we'll use 12:00 noon.) If you have Master Charge or VISA, you may charge your purchase by sending the following information: A. name of your card B. credit card number C. card expiration date.

Mail your orders to the AMERICAN ASTROLOGICAL ASSOCIATION, Research Division, Dept. HH-71, 401 North Market Ave., Canton, Ohio 44750.

Your natal horoscope is covered by a one year — 365 day — full money back guarantee. To avoid a disappointment, why not order your horoscope right now, before you forget. Thanks.